LOEB CLASSICAL MONOGRAPHS

IN MEMORY OF

JAMES C. LOEB

THREE ESSAYS ON
THUCYDIDES

John H. Finley, Jr.

HARVARD UNIVERSITY PRESS

CAMBRIDGE, MASSACHUSETTS · 1967

The Loeb Classical Monographs are
published with assistance from the
Loeb Classical Library Foundation.

Distributed in Great Britain by Oxford University Press, London

Library of Congress Catalog Card Number 67-17308

Printed in the United States of America

PREFACE

❦

These articles concern what, thirty years ago, seemed two chief uncertainties surrounding Thucydides' *History*. The first, which appeared rather from comments of scholars than from formal discussion of the subject, has to do with the cast of Thucydides' style and thought, in the first books especially. If, as some held, it was the joint effect of his exile and of the shock of war to Greek outlooks that bred in him his bold style and the political awareness of which it was the vehicle, then the *History* remains a unique record by a superbly gifted observer, but readers should beware of accepting the picture of the minds and policies, particularly those of Pericles, that he conveyed from the years near the outbreak. Rather, the portrayal would reflect his own slowly matured powers and would be anachronistic in the mouths of men a generation older. The second problem—when the various parts of the *History* may have been composed—had been vehemently pursued since the middle of the last century. It was in some conflict with the first problem: for if Thucydides for a while thought the war over with the Peace of Nicias and wrote much of the first books in that delusion, he would hardly have had time to form new habits of style, and his portrayal of Athenian figures at least would carry fresh memories of the Athens that he left in 424. To be sure, F. W. Ullrich's initial thesis—that the so-called second introduction in V 26 announced the historian's new sense that the several phases of the war comprised one great conflict and hence, to Ullrich's mind, implied that the previous books were written without that understanding—was no longer fully tenable; as was soon pointed out, the first books contain many passages that either expressly mention or evidently assume events at or near the end of the 27-years war. Yet the shadow of the controversy remained, and in the light of it the *History* could be thought not merely truncated at the end but a more or less incomplete compilation throughout. In spite of their contradiction, these two views conspired to cloud understanding of the *History*, since one could not be sure that the author's outlook in the first four books was of a piece with that in the last four, nor, if it was, could one judge how fully to hear in the chief speakers of the first books, not the accent of the times, but the author's voice from some decades later.

Of the two questions, that having to do with the style seemed the easier. If the prose of the late fifth century is largely lost, it was evidently the growth of prose that dictated the progressive change in poetic style from Aeschylus to Euripides. The latter's relative lucidity seems incomprehensible apart from a mounting taste, in his own mind and that of the public, for the effects of order and verisimilitude that prose subserves. Because many dates of Euripidean and other contemporary works are reasonably secure, it is possible to fix with some exactitude the periods when various stylistic usages grew widespread. This question in its relation to Thucydides is the subject of the first two of the following articles.[1] The abundant parallels between

[1] The articles are reprinted with only minor editorial changes from *HSCP* 49 and 50 (1938 and 1939) and from *Athenian Studies Presented to William Scott Ferguson* (*HSCP* Suppl. Vol. 1940). Among desirable changes would be, at p. 90 below, reference to E. Bignone's convincing attempt to distinguish between the two Antiphons ("Antifonte oratore e Antifonte sofista" and "Studi stilistici su Antifonte oratore ed Antifonte sofista," *Rend. Ist. Lomb.* 52, 1919, reprinted in

Preface

Thucydidean speeches in the first books and works from the years in which these were purportedly delivered do not prove that his spokesmen actually used such expressions but show that they might have. It therefore seems certain that he conceived his style as a young man in Athens, not as a mature man in exile, and also that what, for want of a better word, may be called his political realism was not uncharacteristic of the Athens of his youth—on the contrary, carries authentic tones of the years after the Peace of 445 and the Samian revolt when the grip of Athens on the Delian League was hardening.

It is not surprising—rather, the opposite would be surprising—that his mind should thus have borne the stamp of his impressionable years. The statement in V 26.5 that he was of an age to have observed the entire war seems directed against a possible objection that he was either too young at the start or too old at the end to have followed events personally, but since at the end when he was in the full tide of his writing he could hardly have imagined the latter objection, the words suggest that he was in fact relatively young at the outbreak. The impulse to defend himself might otherwise not have occurred to him. One therefore imagines him in early maturity—probably in his twenties—in 431, but the statement of the first sentence of the *History* that he foresaw the magnitude of the impending war shows what he remembered as his then state of awareness. Further,

---

Studi sul Pensiero antico,[1] Napoli, Loffredo, 1938, 161–215; 2nd ed. Roma, Breitschneider, 1965). The argument at p. 4 below and throughout would have been strengthened by G. W. Bowersock's dating of the pseudo-Xenophontic ’Αθηναίων Πολιτεία to approximately 443 (to appear in his forthcoming Loeb edition of the work and in *HSCP* 71). This welcome change from E. Kalinka's dating in the early 420's (Teubner 1913, 5–17) makes clear how a politically minded but not otherwise elaborately educated Athenian wrote during Thucydides' youth. G. Zuntz's *The Political Plays of Euripides* (Manchester 1955) happily corrects some dates of plays from the period of the Archidamian War, notably of the *Suppliants,* suggested at pp. 7–8 below.

if he was by birth a Philaid and kinsman of Cimon and
Thucydides the son of Melesias—as his father's name, his
Thracian connections, and the tradition of his place of burial
join to assert—his admiration of Pericles implies some kind
of political conversion, presumably in the years before the
outbreak. This is of course an inference from the assumed
solidarity of an important family, and one that had suffered
much from Pericles, but even if for reasons that escape us he
was reared in sympathy with the statesman and his policies,
the political traditions of his upbringing were such as to have
prompted early passion for politics.

Without rehearsing here the evidence submitted below
but on the tentative assumption that he in fact carried into
exile the formative stamp of the Athens of his youth, it
follows that readers of the *History* soon after the turn of the
century would have found it an astonishing document. In
the age of Lysias' new Atticism, of Xenophon's unpreten-
tiousness, and of Plato's first efforts at naturalistic dialogue,
its formal antitheses would have breathed a manner thirty
years gone. Dionysius' comment on Aeschylus and Pindar[2]
—that their noble austerity kept an ἀρχαῖος πίνος, as of
the flower on old bronze—might almost have applied to it.
Later generations thought him a pupil of Antiphon the
rhetor, an older man than he, and the *Tetralogies*, which are
ascribed to the 420's, come nearest the style of the speeches.
As Eduard Meyer persuasively argued,[3] the temper of the
work also carried older tones. The historian's defense of
Pericles and his attribution of the defeat to the aggrandizing
policies of later men ran counter to a mood that could
conveniently blame the war on the man who began it.

This archaism of both style and argument must relate to
his exile. Dante, Machiavelli, and (if blindness resembles

[2] *Demosthenes* 39.1074.
[3] *Forschungen zur alten Geschichte* (Halle 1899) II 296-326.

viii

exile) Milton show how intensely minds once immersed in active affairs can ponder their teachings in later isolation. Tacitus' remarks at the start of the *Agricola*, if not wholly germane, convey the mental intensification that accompanies enforced silence. Inner dialogue must tend to sketch its own structures of thought, to condense, regulate, and discover latent meaning in events and words that formerly seemed random. What other form of command remains to an exile? Thucydides checked this tendency to schematism by the care in verifying events of which he speaks in I 22.2–3, also by his search for informants on both sides which he notes in V 26.5. The power of the work derives not least from this tension between his care for detail and his bent toward scheme and structure. In his celebrated article on the speeches, Jebb described the effects of the latter tendency;[4] for example, in the exhortations preceding the second naval engagement on the Gulf of Corinth in the summer of 429 (II 87–89), Phormio counters nearly point by point the grounds of confidence that the Peloponnesian commanders were even then propounding across a few miles of water. Thucydides' paired speeches show in large the analytical parallelism that he brought to his sentences and clauses; his antithetical cast of style is also a cast of thought. But as Euripides', indeed Sophocles', paired speeches make clear, it is this very habit of thought that he acquired in youth in Athens; it is the mark, not of his uniqueness, but of his bond with a place and generation. Though therefore the silences of exile no doubt enhanced this cast of mind as inner dialogue wove the marvelous fabric of his interlocking designs, the process was one of intensifying, not of falsifying, what he had once known. Moreover, there are grades of schematism in the speeches,

4 *Hellenica*², ed. E. Abbott (London 1898) 244–95.

and if the just mentioned exhortations mark one extreme, Pericles' unpaired speeches show an opposite effort to present a single mind. Even there, to be sure, the effort is not total, since parts of the Funeral Oration stand in formal contrast to Archidamus' portrayal in the first book of the Spartan ἀγωγή and outlook (II 39–40, I 83–84). So imperious a mind follows its own laws, which finally evade analysis. But two conclusions seem justified: first, that in the tension between bent toward schematism and care for unique fact, the two forces kept balance and, second, that the speeches of his Athenians, though condensed and though often related antithetically to other speeches, must have seemed to him the more truthful because, as he remembered, the actual speakers used a rhetoric not unlike his own. That cannot have been true of Spartans and other non-Athenians, and in reporting their speeches he, like Homer presenting his Trojans and Herodotus his Persians, yielded to canons of consistency. It is a paradox that speeches of the sixth and seventh books, of Alcibiades especially, must be imagined farthest from their originals, because the trend to the new Atticism—the trend that the historian escaped through his exile—must then have been already under way. By the same token the Athenian speeches of the first four books may be thought most authentic. Beyond his conscious fidelity, expressed in the famous sentence of I 22.1, to the ξύμπασα γνώμη of speeches actually made, lay the unconscious impulse of models emulated in youth, and in the age before Lysias brought to speech-writing his new goals of ἠθοποιία,[5] the standards of that rhetoric cannot have differed much from man to man. Though readers will variously appraise the refracting influence of his schematism and also doubtless of quite personal habits of style, both products of a

[5] Dion. Halic. *Lysias* 8.

long exile, his purpose and the unusual nature of his life jointly confirm his portrayal of the Athens that he had known.

The third article, on the unity of the *History*, tries to show a series of related statements that bind the work together and mark a single, consistent outlook. But even to grant this larger consistency may not solve all questions of date, since uncertainty might remain at what time he became convinced of Athens' ultimate defeat. Yet some practical considerations enter. Though he owed his exile to Cleon's abandonment of the Periclean restraint—since Brasidas would hardly have been allowed to reach Thrace in the summer of 424 and, if he had, Thucydides and his colleague Eucles would have been reinforced, had the Athens of Cleon been less distracted by the abortive Boeotian campaign—and though he thus had early and personal reason to approve Pericles' policy of nonexpansion, it is hard to imagine him then sitting down to write. The shock of exile would have been heavy at first, but even after 421 a resident of Thrace—as tradition held him to have been—would have had small reason for confidence in the Peace of Nicias, since the Spartans kept Amphipolis in violation of the treaty. Alcibiades' Peloponnesian alliance soon followed, and the historian's then interest in these developments seems to speak in the weight that he gives to the battle of Mantinea in 418 (esp. V 72.2, 75.3). Throughout these years he could hardly have believed the war over and the time for writing at hand. Moreover, one of his chief eventual themes, Athens' resilience in defeat, had yet to be evoked. Alcibiades continued active in the next years and the decision to attack Syracuse crowned his policies, but the topographical and other detail of the sixth and seventh books makes as certain as such things can be that Thucydides visited Syracuse,[6]

[6] M. V. Chambers, "Studies in the Veracity of Thucydides," summarized in *HSCP* 62 (1957) 141-43.

necessarily after 413. The account in the eighth book of
Athens' resilience would have led on to the naval victory
at Cyzicus in 410, the rise of Cleophon, and the rejection of
Spartan overtures of peace—a subject of great interest to the
historian, formally broached in the fourth book before
Sphacteria in 425. This rejection, repeated even after
Arginusae in 406, would surely have seemed to him, as
incipiently in IV, a sign of self-interested leadership and
deep political division, hence further proof of the correctness
of Pericles' initial policies. The roster of his themes would
now have been complete, and Athens' defeat must have
seemed to him imminent. He therefore may have turned
steadily to writing in the last years of the war but, if so,
had not finished the extant *History* before the end of his
exile and his return to Athens, since many passages make
clear his knowledge of the full and final defeat.

He certainly kept notes, presumably from the first years
forward, and may early have attempted speeches and
analytical passages; such mastery as his hardly emerges
fully grown. Yet a chief impression of the *History* is of its
tightness of texture; a given passage commonly brings to
mind others, and near-repetition creates the sense of a great
but not limitless store of idea and phrase continually forming
fresh but related designs. It is this internal allusiveness that
chiefly suggests a single sustained period of final composition.
One other characteristic, which seems related to his exile,
may be worth noting: his concentration on the past moment
in hand. His annalistic method fostered this bent of mind,
but it seems prompted by more than procedure only, rather
by a temperament that lived intensely what engaged it. If,
as is argued below, even the Archaeology and, with it, the
opening sentences of the *History* are late passages written
near or after 404, the reason why he did not then mention

the length of the war was that his mind was on the outbreak. The Archaeology is, in function, an extended note or appendix (resembling in this respect the Pentecontaetia) to justify his original prescience by explaining why he judged that the impending war would exceed those of earlier times. His argument carries him backward, not forward, and he seems lost in reliving his memory. It has lately been urged[7] that, writing at the end of the war, he would not have given his present emphasis in the first book to Corinth and Corcyra, which later proved of minor importance; hence that some parts of the account of the outbreak betray an early date. But the great Corinthian speech contrasting Athens to Sparta is of a piece with his whole judgment of the adversaries, and the treatment of Corcyra leads forward to one of the chief themes of the *History*, the political instability that undid many states, including Athens. His rehearsal of these once vivid happenings seems, like the Archaeology, much more easily explicable through the ardor of his backward gaze.

These reasons, among others, may reinforce the argument made below that the *History* is a consistent document apparently reflecting a more or less continuous period of composition, hence necessarily from late in the author's life near the end of the war and after it. But if so and if the related argument on his style is at all acceptable, the resulting conclusion is at first sight surprising: namely, that though Thucydides' style and thought reflect the Athens that he knew before 424, the *History* as we have it dates from some two decades later. His exile explains the seeming contradiction.

I am deeply grateful to our recent and present chairmen, Professors C. H. Whitman and W. V. Clausen, and to our

7 A. Andrewes, "Thucydides on the Causes of the War," *CQ* n. s. 9 (1959) 223–39.

younger colleague, a Thucydidean among his other attainments, Professor G. W. Bowersock, who in their generosity jointly conceived the plan of republishing these old articles. The publication will inaugurate a new series made possible by the bequest of the late James C. Loeb, whose famous gift to establish the Loeb Classical Library has now after many years reverted to Harvard University. For this privilege too I offer feeling thanks.

J.H.F., Jr.

Cambridge, Massachusetts
October 20, 1966

CONTENTS

THREE ESSAYS ON THUCYDIDES

EURIPIDES AND THUCYDIDES

❦

I

Editors have noted, and readers must often feel, resemblances of thought and expression between Euripides' tragedies and the *History* of Thucydides. No extant Euripidean play, except the *Cyclops*, fails to present many such. Nor is the fact surprising. The two men lived for some years in the same city, surveyed throughout their lives the same march of events, and felt the force of the same rhetorical and speculative movements. It is true that Thucydides was in exile from Athens after 424; how old he was at the time is not known. Even if he was a comparatively young man, still he had passed the formative years of his life in the city, and his own statement (I 1) leads us to believe that he elaborated much in exile that he had conceived at home. It is possible that he later met Euripides at the court of Archelaus.[1] So much is at least implied in the doubtful tradition that he wrote the well-known epitaph in the poet's honor.[2]

It is not difficult then to understand why resemblances should exist in the works of the two men. What those resemblances mean and what can be learned from them are

[1] In Marcellinus, 29–30, Thucydides is mentioned with Archelaus and authors known to have been at his court, although not with Euripides. Cf. R. Hirzel, "Die Thukydideslegende," *Hermes* 13 (1878) 46–49.

[2] *Anth. Pal.* VII 45; Athenaeus *Deipn.* V 187e; *Vita Eur.* 40, where Timotheus is also given as author.

questions which present, on the other hand, great difficulties. It is not my purpose here to treat all of the subject, interesting and profitable as it might be to study each man in the light of his agreements with the other. Rather, I have collected relevant passages in the plays and fragments merely for their use in studying the *History*.[3] What will be said of Euripides will be said, therefore, for the exclusive purpose of illuminating the outlook and method of his contemporary.

It will be well to state at the start what problems in the interpretation of Thucydides a comparison with Euripides might help to clarify. The essential problem might be stated thus: if Thucydides, as scholars have maintained, composed his work as a unit in the years about 404 (or to put the matter in another way, if it is extremely difficult to show that any large part of his work was composed many years earlier),[4] and if, in addition, he meant by the famous sentence in I 22.1 that neither in form nor in expression were his speeches intended to be close copies of speeches actually delivered,[5] then what means have we of judging how far he reflects ideas and forms of expression current in Athens as early as 431? The question is important; our whole concept of the intellectual temper of Periclean Athens would be affected if we failed to believe that the speeches in the first and second books, or anything like them, could have been delivered at the start of the war. Yet that view has in effect been upheld. Great weight has, for instance, been placed on the influence

[3] I have used for Thucydides the edition of H. S. Jones, Oxford 1898; for Euripides, the second edition of Gilbert Murray, Oxford 1913; for the fragments, A. Nauck's *Tragicorum Graecorum Fragmenta*[2], Leipzig 1926.

[4] Harald Patzer, "Das Problem der Geschichtsschreibung des Thukydides und die Thukydideische Frage," *Neue deutsche Forschungen*, Abt. klass. Phil., Berlin 1937. But it is unnecessary to reopen here the complex controversy on when Thucydides composed his *History*. Even the advocates of an earlier version admit that much of the work which we have was written after 404.

[5] August Grosskinsky, "Das Programm des Thukydides," *Neue deutsche Forschungen*, Abt. klass. Phil., Berlin 1936.

of Gorgias on Attic prose after his arrival in Athens in 427, and his figure has loomed so large that prose before his time has been thought to be undeveloped. Yet he came to Athens two years after the death of Pericles. Again, Wilamowitz saw in the Peloponnesian War itself the stimulus that gave rise to political thinking.[6] Is then the developed political thought of Thucydides, nowhere more apparent than in the speeches of the first two books, anachronistic in the period from which it purports to emanate? Finally, our knowledge of political oratory in the Periclean Age is so slight and the piety of Sophocles and Herodotus so imposing, that we are slow to believe that anything like the rhetoric or the rationalism of Thucydides can have flourished at that time. And yet we know of Pericles' intimacy with such men as Protagoras, Anaxagoras, and Damon, and feel that so great an upheaval as that caused by the rise of democratic Athens cannot have been unattended by either political theory or political rhetoric.

A comparison between Euripides[7] and Thucydides might therefore give some insight into the question how faithfully Thucydides represents the thought of the years which he describes. For if ideas or forms of argument which the latter puts into the mouths of his speakers appear likewise in the tragedies of Euripides, then it is apparent, not of course that the speakers actually used those ideas or arguments, but that they could have, and that Thucydides is therefore giving a possible picture of men's attitude towards events some of which took place more than a quarter of a century before he himself, in all probability, wrote. Some such accuracy he certainly claimed for his speeches in the

---

[6] *Aristoteles und Athen* (Berlin 1893) I 171–85.

[7] Relevant passages of Sophocles will also be adduced, but since he was less affected than Euripides by the sophistic movement and, as a dramatist, was less addicted to discussing topics of the day, his plays offer fewer parallels to the *History.*

well-known phrase (I 22.1), ἐχομένῳ ὅτι ἐγγύτατα τῆς ξυμπάσης γνώμης τῶν ἀληθῶς λεχθέντων, and again when he remarks of Pericles' first speech (I 145), καὶ τοῖς Λακεδαιμονίοις ἀπεκρίναντο τῇ ἐκείνου γνώμῃ, καθ' ἕκαστά τε ὡς ἔφρασε καὶ τὸ ξύμπαν. The close correspondence, likewise, which has been noted between the pseudo-Xenophontic Ἀθηναίων Πολιτεία[8] and the speeches of Pericles shows that, in a few cases at least, Thucydides attributes to the statesman ideas which were apparently commonplaces in the contemporary discussion of democracy and which, as such, Pericles must have known. If Euripides offers further resemblances of the same kind, then these should give further proof that the historian at the end of the century is not entirely rephrasing in his own way what he conceived to have been the issues of the past, but that he does in fact keep the echo of ideas and arguments once used when those issues were before men. Similarly, resemblances in thought between the early plays of Euripides and parts of the *History* other than the speeches would suggest that the historian was himself influenced by ideas current in Athens before his exile.

But another consideration presents itself to anyone who tries to appraise resemblances in Greek literature, the question, namely, of traditional language. Where similarities exist, it may well be the case that one author is not imitating another nor even that both are following a common source,

---

[8] W. Nestle, "Thukydides und die Sophistik," *Neue Jahrbücher f. d. klass. Altertum* 33 (1914) 649–81, and F. Taeger, *Thukydides* (Stuttgart 1925) 174–88. The comparable passages are: on naval power, II 62.1–3 (cf. I 143.3–144.1, II 65.7), *Ath. Pol.* 2.2–6; on the advantages to Athens of being an island, I 143.5, *Ath. Pol.* 2.14; on trade, II 38.2, *Ath. Pol.* 2.7 and 11; on festivals, II 38.1, *Ath. Pol.* 2.9; on free election to office in a democracy, II 37.1, *Ath. Pol.* 1.2–3; on the ἐμπειρία of Athenians as sailors, I 142.6–143.2 (cf. I 80.4, 121.4, VI 68.2, 69.1, VII 21.3), *Ath. Pol.* 1.19–20; on litigation at Athens, I 77, *Ath. Pol.* 1.16–18; on the tendency of the δῆμος to blame its leaders, I 140.1, II 64.1, *Ath. Pol.* 2.17; on the allies, II 13.2, *Ath. Pol.* 1.14–15; on the wealth of Athens, I 142.1, II 13, *Ath. Pol.* 2.11.

but that they are independently using conventional expressions. Now formal argumentation must have been the rule in the rhetoric of the fifth century. Antiphon repeats himself word for word in different speeches;[9] Aristotle says of Gorgias and the early sophists that they provided their pupils with a limited stock of fixed arguments to be used as the occasion demanded;[10] only with Plato's *Phaedrus*, the Περὶ Σοφιστῶν of Alcidamas, and Isocrates' Κατὰ Σοφιστῶν (XIII) is the formal method of the earlier rhetoric seriously questioned.[11] Thus there is reason to believe that not only Thucydides in his speeches but the original speakers whom he alleges to quote conceived of oratory as following certain fixed rules and using certain lines of argument, more or less well known. It is striking that when he says of his speakers (I 22.1) that he has had them τὰ δέοντα μάλιστ᾽ εἰπεῖν, he is using exactly the words with which Socrates in the *Phaedrus* (234e6) characterizes the older type of argumentation—ὡς τὰ δέοντα εἰρηκότος. And similarly, the rhetoric by which Euripides was influenced must have been of the same formal type. When then Thucydides and Euripides set forth similar ideas, it is a very possible deduction that neither of them is primarily imitating some well-known rhetorician or orator, but on the contrary, like all men who concerned themselves with

---

[9] V 14 = VI 2; V 88–89 = VI 5–6. O. Navarre, who sees in the *Tetralogies* of Antiphon a rhetorical Τέχνη, characterizes its method as "rebaissant l'art de plaider à une tâche presque mécanique." He concludes, "le travail d'invention personnelle se trouvait restreint au strict minimum" (*Essai sur la Rhétorique Grecque* [Paris 1900] 153). Cf. F. Blass, *Die attische Beredsamkeit*[2], (Leipzig 1887) I 121.

[10] *Soph. Elench.* 34.183b36. The passage is quoted below, p. 39.

[11] The three works differ in their exact import. Alcidamas advances reasons why the memorizing of prepared arguments gives insufficient training for actual speaking; in §31, he refers to his own extempore speeches as unusual to his audiences. Isocrates, who likewise ridicules the use of fixed arguments (XIII 10 and 12), judiciously states that oratory demands not only natural gifts but practice and theoretical training (XIII 14–15; cf. Navarre [above, n. 9] 187–207). Plato attacks the older rhetoric on far more philosophical grounds when he says that it fails to depend primarily on logical analysis (*Phaedrus* 265d–266b), and that hence it is repetitious (263a–b) and lacks order and unity (264b–c).

speaking, they are merely following the customary rules of rhetoric. In resemblances between the two one would thus be dealing with the tools, as it were, of fifth-century oratory.

Such considerations cast an interesting light on the speeches of Thucydides. It must never, of course, be forgotten that these are without exception the product of his own style, that they are so intimately tied to one another by cross-references as to play a vital and progressive part in his *History*, and that they are much more compressed than actual speeches would have been. Still, once it be admitted that oratory in the fifth century was conventional, it becomes possible to say that the speeches of Thucydides are his own and yet to contend that they reflect types of thought and of argumentation widely used among his contemporaries. The chief objection to such a line of argument would be based on the view of Wilamowitz cited above: namely, that both rhetoric and political theory developed so fast during the Peloponnesian War that Thucydides actually attributes an anachronistic skill and intellectuality to his speakers. But it is just here that the utility of comparisons with Euripides appears. If he can be shown to use, even in his early plays, forms of conventional argumentation similar to those attributed by Thucydides to his speakers, then we should be justified in considering the latter's speeches as representative of the oratory commonly known even as early as at the outbreak of the war.

Resemblances therefore between Euripides and Thucydides might indicate: first, that the historian was himself influenced by ideas current in Athens before his exile;

then, that he attributes to his speakers ideas and arguments familiar at the time when he represents them as speaking;

finally, that both authors reflect a common rhetorical

tradition which can only be thought of as well known in
Athens and, therefore, as the common ground between
Thucydides and the men whom he represents as speaking.

II

But before approaching the main subject, one should
speak briefly of the dates of Euripides' plays, since the
following argument will often turn on chronology. The
earliest known tragedy is the *Peliades* of 455 (*Vita Eur.*
33); the earliest extant play the *Alcestis* of 438, produced as the
fourth of a tetralogy consisting of the *Cressae, Alcmeon in
Psophis,* and *Telephus* (*Arg. Alc.*). Next is the *Medea* of 431,
produced with the *Philoctetes, Dictys,* and *Theristae,* a satyr
play (*Arg. Med.*). These tragedies then appeared before the
outbreak of the war, and to them must be added the
Hippolytus Kaluptomenos[12] and doubtless some, although
we do not know which, of the plays mentioned in
Acharnians 418–34, namely, the *Oeneus, Phoenix, Bellerophon,
Thyestes,* and *Ino* (I omit the *Telephus* and *Philoctetes,*
already mentioned). The only dated play during the Archidamian War is the *Hippolytus* of 428 (*Arg. Hipp.*), but the
Heraclidae was probably produced shortly after its outbreak
and the *Andromache* and *Hecuba* a few years later.[13] Near the
close of the war appeared the *Erechtheus*;[14] the *Suppliants*
followed the Peace of Nicias, either directly or, as seems
more probable, in 420 or 419.[15] The *Heracles,* dated by

[12] M. Pohlenz, *Die griechische Tragödie* (Leipzig 1930) 258.

[13] Cf. the chronological notes on these plays in Murray's edition; also the
introductions to the same in the edition of L. Méridier ("Collections des Universités
de France," Paris, I, 1925; II, 1927) I 195, II 106 and 179.

[14] Cf. U. von Wilamowitz-Moellendorff, *Euripides Herakles*[2] (Berlin 1933) 134,
and L. Parmentier and H. Grégoire, *Euripide* (a continuation of the edition of L.
Méridier, noted above; III, 1923; IV, 1925) III 98.

[15] The earlier date is advocated by Wilamowitz and by Parmentier and Grégoire;
see above, n. 14. The argument in favor of the later date, in my opinion very
strong (see below, p. 37), is set forth by G. H. Macurdy, *The Chronology of the
Extant Plays of Euripides* (Columbia diss. 1905) 55.

7

Wilamowitz shortly after the *Suppliants*,[16] has been placed
by Zielinski on metrical grounds with what he calls the
plays of the free style, composed after 415.[17] He ascribes the
Ion to the same group,[18] although historical references in
the play seem to point to the year 418.[19] No doubt attaches
at least to the tetralogy of 415, the *Alexander*, *Palamedes*,
Trojan Women, and *Sisyphus* (Aelian *Var. Hist.* II 8). The
order then seems with some certainty to be, *Iphigenia
among the Taurians* 414–413, *Electra* 413, *Helen* and *Andro-
meda* 412.[20] The *Phoenissae* was probably produced in 409,
perhaps in the same tetralogy with the *Hypsipyle* and
Antiope,[21] the *Orestes* following in the next year. Finally,
the *Iphigenia at Aulis*, *Alcmeon in Corinth*, and *Bacchae* were
produced after the poet's death (Schol. Ar. *Ran.* 64), the
first suffering then or later many additions.[22]

This list, it need hardly be said, is incomplete, and it does
far less than justice to many problems of date and order. It
is given for convenience and largely to remind the reader
what plays were produced before and during the Archidamian War. For most of these go back to the years when
Thucydides knew Athens and give evidence for the thought
of the times. I turn now to the parallels between the two
authors, treating them by the books of the *History*.

Euripides echoes a few of the facts cited by the historian
in the Archaeology: that the Athenians, unlike other
peoples, has always inhabited their country (I 2.5–6; *Erech.*
fg. 360, *Ion* 589–93, 673), that they had settled Ionia (I 2.6;
Ion 1578–88), and that in early times the sons of Hellen had

[16] Page 135; see above, n. 14.
[17] *Tragodumenon, Libri Tres* (Cracoviae 1925) 185.
[18] So also Pohlenz (above, n. 12) *Erläuterungen*, 123.
[19] Parmentier and Grégoire (above, n. 14) III 168.
[20] See the chronological notes in Murray's edition.
[21] J. U. Powell, *The Phoenissae of Euripides* (London 1911) 34–38.
[22] D. L. Page, *Actors' Interpolations in Greek Tragedy*, Oxford 1934.

been called in to assist states (I 3.2; *Ion* 59–64). Far more instructive is it that Thucydides' method of using τεκμήρια to establish uncertain events (I 1.3, 20.1, 21.1) is described in a line of the *Phoenix* (fg. 811),[23]

τἀφανῆ τεκμηρίοισιν εἰκότως ἁλίσκεται.

The method, closely allied as it is to the rhetorical principle of εἰκός elaborated by the Sicilians Corax and Tisias, may have become known in Athens through Protagoras, who visited Sicily and went as a lawgiver to Thurii in 443.[24] The latter principle is, at all events, well illustrated in another fragment of the *Phoenix* (fg. 812) which, after stating that you can judge a man by observing his φύσις and his way of life, concludes

τοιοῦτός ἐστιν οἷσπερ ἥδεται ξυνών.[25]

It is hardly necessary to point out how greatly Thucydides relies on these principles of τεκμήρια and εἰκός when he deduces a course of history from Homer's description of men's habits in former times.[26] And although it is only in a late play (*Archelaus* fg. 261) that Euripides expresses in so many words what is perhaps the fundamental law of the Archaeology, namely, that the strong control the weak for their mutual advantage, his early plays abound in ideas of a similar cast. One might cite the remark of the Paedagogus which sets the whole tone of Jason's character in the *Medea* (85–86),

ἄρτι γιγνώσκεις τόδε,
ὡς πᾶς τις αὑτὸν τοῦ πέλας μᾶλλον φιλεῖ,[27]

[23] See also the saying of Pericles, quoted below, p. 54. J. T. Lees (Δικανικὸς Λόγος *in Euripides*, Johns Hopkins diss. 1891, 41) gives the following passages as illustrating Euripides' use of τεκμήρια: *Alc.* 634, 653; *Andr.* 677; *Elec.* 1041, 1086; *Hec.* 1206; *Hel.* 920; *Hcld.* 142; *I.A.* 1185; *Tro.* 961, 962, 970.

[24] Navarre, *Rhétorique Grecque*, 21–23.

[25] J. T. Lees (above, n. 23) cites the use of the argument from εἰκός in the following passages: *Bacch.* 288; *Elec.* 947, 1036; *Hec.* 271, 282, 1207; *Her.* 1314; *Ion* 594–611; *Hipp.* 1008; *Orest.* 532.

[26] E. Täubler, *Die Archaeologie des Thukydides* (Leipzig 1927) 103–7.

[27] Cf. I 8.3 where it is said that the strong and the weak made common cause in early times, both equally ἐφιέμενοι τῶν κερδῶν.

or the lines from what is probably an even earlier play
(*Hipp. Kal.* fg. 434),

οὐ γὰρ κατ' εὐσέβειαν αἱ θνητῶν τύχαι,
τολμήμασιν δὲ καὶ χερῶν ὑπερβολαῖς
ἁλίσκεταί τε πάντα καὶ θηρεύεται.

These ideas, although not identical with those expounded
in the Archaeology, reflect at least the same realistic attitude
toward human motives.

When in I 20–23 the historian criticizes his predecessors,
states the methods and aims of his own work, and contrasts
the latent with the superficial causes of the war, he again
touches the thought of Euripides in several ways. The latter's
criticism of Aeschylus is well known (*Elec.* 524–44, *Suppl.*
846–57, *Phoen.* 751–52), but it is worth observing that in the
first of these passages he finds fault with his predecessor's
criteria and, in the second, states the extreme difficulty of
learning what takes place in the course of a battle—ideas
to which Thucydides gave a special and quite technical
importance. There can be no question of influences here;
Euripides is merely expressing in small details that critical
and rationalistic spirit which he reveals in far more searching
ways in such characters as Pheres, Jason, and Electra. All
the more then do these detailed resemblances in the thought
of the two men appear to reflect a more widespread
rationalism which, since it is evident in the poet's early
plays, must not be considered as resulting from the war
alone. The well-known statement of Sophocles in which he
contrasted his art with that of his younger rival (*Arist.
Poet.* 25.1460b33) could, in fact, have been said almost as
appropriately by Herodotus of Thucydides. When it is
remembered that that contrast applies entirely to what we
know of Euripides' early plays, then it seems at least possible
that Thucydides also acquired his critical and innovating

outlook before the beginning of the war when, he says (I 1),
he already thought of writing his *History*.

The cyclic view of life by which Thucydides justifies the
usefulness of his book appears likewise in the *Ino* (fg. 415),
but a more important resemblance to the thought of I 22
is suggested by what the historian says there of his speeches.
He remarks that he has caused his speakers to express
especially what in his own opinion would be demanded
under the successive circumstances, while at the same time
he has kept as close as possible to the general import of
what was actually said. When one turns to the speeches
themselves, it is clear that Thucydides meant by the phrase
"what would be demanded"—τὰ δέοντα—those broad
considerations, material, social, and psychological in nature,
by which men form their own or others' judgment on
specific topics. And without anticipating here what will be
better discussed under the different speeches,[28] one can at
least say that Euripides also conceived his debates in a
similar spirit. Contrasting the latter's *Philoctetes* with those
of Aeschylus and Sophocles, Dio Chrysostom (*Orat.* 52.
11 and 13) felt that it was written μετὰ πάσης ἐν τῷ
εἰπεῖν δυνάμεως; the prologue in which Odysseus announ-
ces a coming embassy of Trojans served as ἀνευρίσκων
λόγων ἀφορμάς, καθ᾽ ἃς εἰς τἀναντία ἐπιχειρῶν εὐπορώ-
τατος καὶ παρ᾽ ὁντινοῦν ἱκανώτατος φαίνεται. Much the
same judgment could be made of the debate in the contemporary *Medea* (446–575), in which both Medea and Jason
expound those broad considerations of human nature and
human experience by which their own acts can be justified
and the other's condemned. Thucydides' plan for his speeches
has then much in common with the rhetorical practice of
Euripides in his early plays. And when the historian in I 23

[28] See below, pp. 17–18, 22–24, 30–35, 40–44, 49–50.

goes on to distinguish between the superficial and the real causes of the war, he makes in large a distinction which Euripides several times makes in small (*Andr.* 391–93, *Elec.* 1040, *I.A.* 938–40).

We come now to the speeches, the first of which, that of the Corcyreans at Athens (I 32–36), turns on the argument that the Athenians will be wise to prepare for the inevitable war by allying themselves with another naval power καὶ προεπιβουλεύειν αὐτοῖς μᾶλλον ἢ ἀντεπιβουλεύειν (I 33.4). They further state that it will be just for Athens to do so, an argument opposed by the Corinthians (I 39–40) and from the foregoing account (esp. I 25–26) apparently doubtful, on purely moral grounds, to Thucydides. Their plea recalls the words of Creon in the *Medea* (349–51), that it is a weakness to be turned from your material interests by moral scruples, and again (289), that one must anticipate evils by action,

ταῦτ᾽ οὖν πρὶν παθεῖν φυλάξομαι.

Like Jason in the same play (548–50), the envoys state at the start what they must prove (I 32.1); in both cases also, the argument turns on personal advantage clothed in the terms of justice. Again, like the Mytileneans pleading for Spartan help (III 9), they seek to forfend ill opinion by explaining why they have deserted their natural ties (I 34),[29] a form of reasoning which brings to mind Electra's words on the dead Aegisthus (*Elec.* 918–24), that he should have judged his wife's future by her past conduct. In the *Medea* (869–905) Jason to his cost is thus convinced of his wife's change of heart. In short, the *Medea* shows Euripides to be fully aware not only of the lines of argument, τὸ συμφέρον and

[29] Cf. *Rhet. ad Alex.* 1424b36, δεῖ δέ, ὅταν συναγορεύειν βούλῃ τῇ γινομένῃ συμμαχίᾳ, ... δεικνύναι τοὺς τὴν συμμαχίαν ποιουμένους μάλιστα μὲν δικαίους ὄντας. The treatise professes to rely in part on the teachings of Corax (1421b2) and thus may in some cases reproduce arguments known in Athens during the Periclean Age (see above, p. 9).

τὸ δίκαιον, on which the Corcyreans base their appeal, but also of the formal use of those arguments in speeches. Medea appealing to Jason and, later, Jason to Medea have, like the envoys, "dressed their utterance well" (*Med.* 576); beneath, in all three cases, are entirely material ends.

I omit the first speech of the Corinthians at Sparta (I 68–71); for although the contrast there made between Spartan ἡσυχία and Athenian πολυπραγμοσύνη is well known in Euripides, it may best be discussed under later speeches. After the Corinthians, the Athenians come forward "to remind the old and instruct the young" (I 72.1; cf. *Suppl.* 842–43) and, like Adrastus in the *Suppliants* (253), state that they are not speaking as before judges. After rehearsing the feats of Athens in the Persian wars, a subject necessarily absent from Euripides but, to judge by Pericles' dismissal of it μακρηγορεῖν ἐν εἰδόσιν οὐ βουλόμενος (II 36.4), evidently common at the time, they proceed to justify the Athenian empire, first, as involving peril for themselves if it were abandoned and, second, as natural since men subdue what fails to resist (I 75–76). Euripides offers no such exact parallel to either idea as does a fragment of Democritus to the latter, φύσει τὸ ἄρχειν οἰκήιον τῷ κρέσσονι.[30] But the praise of the βίος ἀκίνδυνος (*Ion* 597, 621–47; *Antiope* fgs. 193–94, 198; *I.A.* 16–27; cf. also Soph. *O.T.* 577–602) as well as the statements of the dangers which surround power (*Her.* 65–66; fg. 850) are ideas closely related to the first; still more so is the import of the following fragment (*Hipp. Kal.* 433),

ἔγωγε φημὶ καὶ νόμον γε μὴ σέβειν
ἐν τοῖσι δεινοῖς τῶν ἀναγκαίων πλέον.

It is remarkable that Euripides seems nowhere to expound

30 Diels-Kranz, *Die Fragmente der Vorsokratiker*⁹ (Berlin 1959) II 200, fg. 267.

the "natural right" of the strong.[31] He is familiar, at least, with the doctrine that convention fetters men (*Cycl.* 338–41) and several times says that power knows no moral inhibitions.[32] A conspicuous trait of language in this speech is the repeated use of a series of three general nouns; their empire, say the Athenians, is justifiable through δέος, τιμή, and ὠφελία (I 75.3, 76.2; cf. I 74.1, 122.4, III 40.2). If *Heraclidae* 238–42 and *Medea* 548–49 are perhaps not exact parallels, the formal resemblance to the Τριαγμός of Ion of Chios is striking, πάντα τρία καὶ οὐδὲν πλέον ἢ ἔλασσον τούτων τῶν τριῶν ... σύνεσις καὶ κράτος καὶ τύχη (*Vorsokr.*[9] I 379, fg. 1).

The aged king Archidamus, after advancing reasons for delaying the war, answers the Corinthians' criticism of the Spartan ἡσυχία by setting the trait in a more favorable light and by showing how it is rooted in the Spartan system of discipline (I 83–85). Superficial resemblances to Euripides exist in his appeal to the coolness and experience of the older Spartans (I 80.1; *Bellerophon* fg. 291, *Suppl.* 476–85), in his statement that the strength of Athens is in her allies (I 81.4; *Ion* 1584–85), and in his remark that intellect impedes action (I 84.3; *Peliades* fg. 610). But the part of the speech which touches the thought of Periclean Athens most closely is his description of the Spartan ἀγωγή. Thucydides saw it as a profound contrast to the Athenian way of life expounded in the Funeral Oration: the one relied on discipline and strict observance of law, because, as Archidamus says (I 84.4), men being much alike, those trained in the severest school are most effective; the other, although essentially controlled by law, especially the unwritten laws (II 37.3), trusted its citizens to think and act without recourse to constant

---

[31] But see W. Nestle, *Euripides* (Stuttgart 1901) 203.
[32] Cf. pp. 10, 12, 29, 40–41.

discipline (II 39.3, 40.3). Now this contrast between authoritarian and liberal government must have been very seriously debated at Athens; it is, in fact, at the root of any possible theory of democracy. Aeschylus foreshadowed it when he made the Eumenides threaten that the loss of their power, involved as that loss was with the change in status of the Areopagus, meant the decline of all discipline (*Eum.* 490–565). But the *Ajax* and *Antigone* of Sophocles first discuss the question in the form of antithetical debate made familiar in Athens through Protagoras.[33] In the former play (1073–80), Menelaus, in forbidding Teucer to bury the dead Ajax, enforces his demands on the grounds that law cannot endure without δέος,

> οὔτ' ἂν στρατός γε σωφρόνως ἄρχοιτ' ἔτι
> μηδὲν φόβου πρόβλημα μηδ' αἰδοῦς ἔχων ...
> δέος γὰρ ᾧ πρόσεστιν αἰσχύνη θ' ὁμοῦ
> σωτηρίαν ἔχοντα τόνδ' ἐπίστασο.

Creon (*Antig.* 666–76) likewise thinks civil obedience the school of military discipline. And it is striking how close these passages are to the thought of Archidamus who, like Menelaus, represents discipline as resulting from αἰδώς and σωφροσύνη inculcated by the state and, in his brief speech to the troops early in Book II, lays weight on δέος (II 11.4–5). His insistence on unquestioning obedience to law (I 84.3) recalls especially the first lines of the passage cited from the *Antigone*, and Euripides echoes the point in the *Orestes* when, after making it clear that Tyndareus is a Spartan (457, 537), he portrays him as a legalist (491–541).

On the whole, however, the contrast appears in a different but closely related guise to Euripides. In the *Iphigenia at*

---

33 For the *Antilogies* of Protagoras, see *Vorsokr.*⁹ II 254.7; 255.4; 259.25; 266.1,3. He professed to teach knowledge of government (Plato *Protag.* 318e6), and Aristoxenus saw in his *Antilogies* the substance of Plato's *Republic* (*Vorsokr.*⁹ II 265–66).

Aulis, 558–72, it is stated that training (τροφαί) is chiefly instrumental in producing ἀρετή. But Euripides was not always so sure of the value of training; in the earlier *Hecuba*, 592–602, and *Phoenix*, fg. 810 (cf. *Elec.* 390, 941–42), he states his chief confidence in men's native powers, and one is possibly justified in explaining this change of attitude by the poet's growing conservatism and by the disillusionment with democracy which he felt towards the end of his life.[34] For that, in contemporary theory, democracy implied a trust and oligarchy a distrust of man's native capacities appears not only from the opposing views of Pericles and Archidamus, but from such other contrasts as that between the ἀκρίβεια of the aristocrats and the ἀταξία of the poor in the pseudo-Xenophontic Ἀθηναίων Πολιτεία (1.5), between the αἰδώς of the older generation and the self-indulgence of the younger in the *Clouds* (992, 1077), between the restrained knowledge of the few and the ignorant wildness of the many in the debate among the Persians (Herod. III 81). These last passages are unfavorable to the free ways fostered by democracy, but arguments were made on the other side, one of which seems to have centered about the ἄγραπτοι νόμοι. It is, at least, a striking coincidence that the unwritten laws are cited by Pericles as especially regarded in a democracy (II 37.3), appear as the sanction of Theseus' conduct in the *Suppliants*,[35] and are Antigone's chief support against the oligarchic Creon (*Antig.* 450–60).[36]

[34] Wilamowitz, *Einleitung in die griechische Tragödie*² (Berlin 1921) 14–15.

[35] Theseus speaks, not of the "unwritten laws," but of the νόμος παλαιὸς δαιμόνων (*Suppl.* 563; cf. 311, 526). Andocides, I 85–87, cites a law forbidding judicial decisions based on an ἀγράφῳ νόμῳ. But he is referring to laws not included in the written code of 403, and the words therefore have an entirely different meaning from those under discussion.

[36] It is perhaps worth reminding the reader that the play won Sophocles the office of general (*Arg. Antig.*) at a time when the rivalry of Pericles and Thucydides the son of Melesias had raised serious questions concerning the nature of Attic democracy (see the article of H. T. Wade-Gery cited below, n. 47). It is likely, therefore, that the play conveyed political overtones to the audience.

The argument may have run somewhat as follows: although democracy lacks the strict νόμοι of oligarchy, democratic man with his freer trust in himself feels instinctive accord with the great natural laws. But the point need not be pressed; certainly there were other arguments in favor of democracy as having written laws available for all (II 37.1–3; *Suppl.* 443). It is enough for our purpose if it be accepted that the difference between democracy and oligarchy was analyzed in the years when Thucydides knew Athens and that in introducing into the debate the related questions of strict obedience and freedom, training and natural inclination, distrust and trust of human nature, he is true to the thought of the time.

The second speech of the Corinthians at Sparta need not long detain us. There exists a close parallel to *Bellerophon*, fg. 287,

τοῖς πράγμασιν γὰρ οὐχὶ θυμοῦσθαι χρεών·
μέλει γὰρ αὐτοῖς οὐδέν· ἀλλ' οὑντυγχάνων
τὰ πράγματ' ὀρθῶς ἢν τιθῇ, πράσσει καλῶς,

when, speaking of the unexpectedness of war, the envoys conclude ἐν ᾧ ὁ μὲν εὐοργήτως αὐτῷ προσομιλήσας βεβαιότερος, ὁ δ' ὀργισθεὶς περὶ αὐτὸν οὐκ ἐλάσσω πταίει (I 122.1). And the statement that men do not in action measure up to their previous plans (I 120.5) is common in somewhat differing contexts in Euripides (*I.T.* 729–30, *Alc.* 671–72, *Ion* 585). In form, this speech is a very simple example of a συμβουλευτικός, the first and last paragraphs being exhortation (I 120 and 124), while the second and third show respectively that it is possible for the Peloponnesians to win and at all events shameful for them not to make the attempt.[37] The two topics of possibility (τὸ δυνατόν) and

---

[37] Cf. *Rhet. ad Alex.* 1425a17, ὅταν μὲν οὖν ἐπὶ τὸ πολεμεῖν παρακαλῶμεν ... δεικτέον, ἐξ ὧν ἔστι περιγενέσθαι τῷ πολέμῳ.

honor (τὸ καλόν) are prominent in the *Rhetoric to Alexander* (1421b21–33), and a good example of the use of the latter by Euripides is *Suppliants* 306–19. The former topic is by nature nearly identical with the argument from εἰκός (*Ion* 585–620), and it is worth noting that, if that argument must look to the past in dicanic speeches such as Antiphon's first *Tetralogy* or the self-defense of Hippolytus (*Hipp.* 991–1035; cf. Soph. *O.T.* 577–602), it looks of course chiefly to the future in deliberative speeches.[38] Now a glance at the passage cited from the *Ion*, where the boy surveys the possible dangers awaiting him if he returns with Xuthus to Athens, shows how closely allied is this future use of εἰκός with the πρόγνωσις which Thucydides thought the chief quality of statesmen (I 138.3, II 65.5 and 13). In practice, a statesman undoubtedly showed his πρόγνωσις by expounding what was likely to result from a given step.[39]

The speech of Pericles with which the book ends is similar in plan to the preceding except that, after a short introduction (I 140.1), he speaks briefly of the justice of the war (I 140.2–141.1) and, most appropriately in one whose foresight Thucydides considered supreme, then canvasses at much greater length the prospects of victory (I 141.2–143). Such detailed weighing of chances is foreign to tragedy, but when Pericles states that the essential reason for war is to make clear that Athens will not be commanded by another power, we must believe that this reason was actually the common explanation of the war in most men's minds, since it is a chief theme of the *Heraclidae* (197–201, 286–87, 362–63)

---

[38] Cf. the well-known passage of Aristotle's *Rhetoric* (I 1358b14) in which he specifies the times appropriate to the three classes of oratory: χρόνοι δὲ ἑκάστου τούτων εἰσὶ τῷ μὲν συμβουλεύοντι ὁ μέλλων (περὶ γὰρ τῶν ἐσομένων συμβουλεύει ἢ προτρέπων ἢ ἀποτρέπων). Even epideictic orators sometimes look to the future, τὰ μέλλοντα προεικάζοντες.

[39] Demosthenes (*De Cor.* 246, cf. 189) describes the task of the ῥήτωρ as ἰδεῖν τὰ πράγματα ἀρχόμενα καὶ προαισθέσθαι καὶ προειπεῖν τοῖς ἄλλοις.

and of the *Suppliants* (517–23). An echo of the statesman's figurative style may remain in his remark that events go no less foolishly than the minds of men (I 141.1), a figure repeated in the outcry of Hecuba (*Tro.* 1205) that fortune moves ἔμπληκτος ὡς ἄνθρωπος.

Before leaving the first book we may pause to consider one other subject in which the thought of the poet and of the historian is in close accord, namely, the Spartan character. Something was said of it under the speech of Archidamus in which Thucydides expounds its social origins, but he often recurs to the subject both in the speeches and in his own words, and although it is impossible to treat the shades of his meaning here, one can at least note his main points. The Spartans are slow to act (I 70, 118.2, 132.5; IV 55.2; V 63.2; VIII 96.5), fearful (I 23.6, 88, 90.1; IV 55.2), suspicious of others (I 68.2, 90.2, 102.3, 120.2; III 13.1), and chary in revealing their motives (I 90.2, 102.2). Hence in spite of their great reputation both as warriors and as men of honor (I 132.5, III 57.1, V 105.4), they are bitterly attacked as sunk in their own way of life (I 71.2), cowardly (I 83, V 75.3), and double-faced (V 105.4). That Thucydides thought of them as in fact supremely guided by self-interest appears not only from the biting statement of the Melian Dialogue (V 105.4), ἐπιφανέστατα ὧν ἴσμεν τὰ μὲν ἡδέα καλὰ νομίζουσι, τὰ δὲ ξυμφέροντα δίκαια, but from his judgment of the real causes of the war (I 23.6, 88) and of the trial at Plataea (III 68.4–5). Now Euripides echoes certain of these opinions, notably in Adrastus' characterization (*Suppl.* 187),

Σπάρτη μὲν ὠμὴ καὶ πεποίκιλται τρόπους,

and in Andromache's longer and fiercer invective (*Andr.* 445–63). Her question

οὐ λέγοντες ἄλλα μὲν
γλώσσῃ, φρονοῦντες δ᾽ ἄλλ᾽ ἐφευρίσκεσθ᾽ ἀεί;

19

repeats the historian's judgment of their conduct at the time of the rebuilding of the Athenian walls (I 90.2) and at Ithome (I 102.3). Her allusion to their plight when forced into naval warfare parallels his opinion (I 18.3, IV 55.2; cf. ps.-Xen. *Ath. Pol.* 2.1), and her outcry that they are unjustly famous in Greece, repeated earlier in the play (319–24) and in the *Heraclidae* (745–47), recalls not only the criticisms cited above but the historian's essential idea that, had Athens followed the plan of Pericles, she would have replaced Sparta's outmoded leadership. Their slow secretiveness contrasts with the open vigor of Athens (I 70; *Suppl.* 320–25), their ἡσυχία with her πολυπραγμοσύνη, points on which more will be said under the following speeches of Pericles. And although it is true that, writing war plays for popular hearing, Euripides is often led to blacken Sparta and those whom he portrays as Spartans (for example, Menelaus in the *Andromache* and again, with Tyndareus and Helen, in the *Orestes*), and although he represents Athens as the idealistic protectress of the weak (*Hcld.* 329–32, 757; *Suppl.* 337; and Theseus in the *Her.*), whereas Thucydides regards alliances in the cold light of policy, still even the latter feels that Athens at her best had a vigor and a generosity (II 40.5) which contrasts markedly with the cold and covert self-interest of Sparta. His *History* therefore analyzes and in many ways confirms what Athenians thought of Sparta early in the war. One could go farther and say that it is incorrect to imagine, as some have done,[40] that Thucydides wrote his *History* chiefly to exonerate Pericles when, at the end of the war, his policies seemed to have ruined Athens. For since Thucydides states that he contemplated his work at the start of the war and is seen, as in the case just discussed, to have kept in mind certain issues as they were then pre-

---

[40] E. Schwartz, *Die Geschichtsschreibung des Thukydides*² (Bonn 1929) 133.

sented, it is far easier to believe that, even at the beginning, he saw much that was at stake and spent his life observing and testing the original issues.

With the speeches of Pericles and the historian's judgment of him in the second book we pass from the Spartan government and character, which have much occupied us hitherto, to the Athenian. Euripides not unnaturally mentions the latter constantly; the *Suppliants*, in particular, is almost as enlightening as a friendly exposition of democratic theory as is the tract of the Old Oligarch as an attack upon it. Thus the connection between Euripides and Thucydides is very close for this part of the latter's work and continues to be so through the debate of Cleon and Diodotus in the third book.

Plutarch (*Per.* 8) quotes a phrase from an earlier oration delivered by Pericles after the Samian War, and in II 35.1 the statesman begins by referring to those who had spoken on such occasions in the past. The practice of delivering orations over the fallen must therefore have been familiar, and it is not surprising that Euripides should introduce such a speech into the *Suppliants* (857–917), with the same purpose of public instruction (909–17) as that expressed by Pericles (II 36.4, 43.4–6). A speech exactly opposite in character but with the same didactic purpose is delivered by Electra over the dead Aegisthus (*Elec.* 907–56).[41] In all three cases the subject is the way of life—in the Funeral Oration, the way of life of a whole city—through which the dead came to act as they did. References to the common grave (II 43.2; *Erechtheus* fg. 360.33), free offering of life to the city (II 43; *Phoen.* 1013–18), love of it (II 43.1; *Erech.* fg. 360.54), children as its protectors (II 44.3; *Erech.* 360.14–17;

---

[41] Τὸ ἐγκωμιαστικόν and τὸ ψεκτικόν are treated as the two main divisions of epideictic oratory in *Rhet. ad Alex.* 1425b36.

Ion 483–84), the immortality of noble death (II 43.2–3; *Erech.* 361), offer superficial parallels. That the fame of women is to avoid fame is said by both (II 45.2; *Tro.* 647–50), and like the Funeral Oration, the long fragment 360 already cited from the *Erechtheus* begins by referring to the purity of the autochthonous Athenian stock. But a deeper kinship exists in the exposition of democratic theory. Like Pericles (II 37), Theseus in the *Suppliants* (403–8) speaks of the rule of the demos, of the equality of rich and poor in office and before the law (433–34), and of the distinction accorded to those who can benefit the state (438–41). More significant is it that when Pericles states his firm confidence in debate and in the capacity of all citizens both to interest themselves in the city and to think clearly of its affairs (II 40.2), he is answering exactly the arguments which the Theban Herald in the *Suppliants* (409–25) makes against democracy. The latter says that the oratory of politicians leads the masses astray and that the poor in any case lack the time and ability for politics. Now of these two objections, the second appears in the debate on constitutions (Herod. III 81.2) and is subtly treated by the Old Oligarch, who states that, although the κακοί cannot make right decisions, still their vicious counsels are in their own interest, since good plans would favor the good, that is, the aristocrats (*Ath. Pol.* 1.7–8). Clearly then the question was crucial in the contemporary debate on democracy, and when Pericles defends the fitness of the masses for government, one must see in his words not merely the faith of a convinced democrat but the line of argument actually pursued in the Periclean Age by the advocates of a democratic system.

Other considerations should make the point more clear. We have seen that Pericles states his confidence not only in the masses but in debate, while the Theban Herald sees in the oratory of the demagogues the greater danger to democracy. Thucydides thought exactly that. In the contest between Cleon and Diodotus, he represents the latter as well aware of the danger of ignorance, dishonesty, and διαβολή, yet still true to the Periclean ideal of serious debate (III 42.2); Cleon, on the other hand, the master of διαβολή, opposes real deliberation and taxes the Athenians with an empty love of words. The contest is doubtless meant to convey the increasing difficulty of honest and profitable debate in the assembly. For, speaking of the successors of Pericles, Thucydides says that none far outshone the others but all vied to gratify the demos for their personal ends (II 65.7–10; cf. III 82.8). Herein he sees the chief reason for Athens' defeat (II 65.7–11; VI 15.3–4, 29.3). He clearly felt that Pericles' confidence in the popular judgment proved unfounded in the light of later events, and he therefore welcomed the narrower democracy briefly instituted in 411 (VIII 97.2). The same opposite judgments on oratory appear in Euripides. Theseus in the *Suppliants* and *Heracles* and Erechtheus, as we see him in the two long fragments 360 and 362, are portrayed as political orators in the fullest sense of which Aristotle uses the term of older tragedy (*Poet.* 1450b7). Yet in as early a play as the *Medea*, Jason, an accomplished pleader, uses words only to deceive; the *Suppliants* (229–37) refers to the ruinous self-interest of the younger politicians in exactly the way in which Thucydides speaks of the demagogues in general and of Alcibiades in particular (II 65, VI 15); the διαβολή referred to by the Theban Herald (*Suppl.* 411–16) echoes Thucydides' and Aristophanes' judgment of Cleon (V 16; *Ach.* 380, 502; *Eq.* 710); and the *Palamedes*, *Orestes*, and *Iphigenia at Aulis* show the popular orators in an increasingly venal and vicious light. Besides self-interest, hope, passion, and desire are represented by both authors as misleading.[42] And since reason then seems so beset by dangers, both authors, like Aristotle in the *Rhetoric*, see in a man's ἀξίωμα a force ultimately more persuasive than words (II 65.8; *Hec.* 293–94). Now although the figure of Jason in the *Medea* warns us against blaming the war alone for this breakdown of confidence in reasoned debate, there can be no doubt that, as Thucydides says (III 82.8), war and covert revolution greatly hastened the process. It follows, therefore, that when Pericles justifies reasoned debate as both necessary and possible in democratic Athens, he is stating, as the objections of the Theban Herald in the *Suppliants* clearly show, a vital article in the theory of democracy of his own times. Both Thucydides and Euripides lost faith in debate, although both, it must be added, were molded intellectually by it. Thus in this respect also the Funeral Oration conveys, not the opinion of Thucydides, but the thought of the older Athens of his youth.

Finally, when Pericles says that the poor, although not despised as such, should struggle to escape their poverty (II 40.1), he is at one with the *Suppliants* (177–78, 238–45) and the *Erechtheus* (fg. 362.11–15). And his concluding words that that city is best served which rewards virtue most generously give the theme for a speech in the *Hecuba* (299–331, esp. 306–8; cf. *Rhes.* 161–63, and Soph. *O.T.* 879–80). Thus these ideas too were evidently common in the older democracy. In fact, they comport well with the bracing and optimistic trust in human nature which is not less characteristic of Theseus in the *Suppliants* (195–218) than of Pericles, and which, as we have seen, is fundamentally opposed to the less hopeful Spartan outlook. The city which

---

[42] I 140.1; II 62.5; III 39.3, 97.2; IV 108.4; V 103; *Her.* 309–10, *Med.* 1078–80, *Hipp.* 382, *Chrysippus* fg. 841.

offered this freedom of opportunity prided itself, as Pericles says in a famous sentence (II 41.1), on the wisdom and versatile grace of its citizens. Just such a claim for it is made by Euripides in a hardly less famous chorus of the *Medea* (824–45), sung a few months before the war began and less than a year before Pericles delivered his Funeral Oration. The *Heraclidae*, produced not long after, repeats the boast (379–80).

The historian represents Pericles as speaking a third time to cheer the citizens who now repented of the war, being dejected by a second, more severe invasion and by the plague. If the speech is narrower in purpose than the Funeral Oration, it is, in a sense, as searching in its exposition, first, of the unity necessary within a state, then, of Athens' justified hopes of keeping and later extending her empire through her navy, and finally, of the nature of empire itself. The second part of the speech, although necessarily without parallel in Euripides, is shown to be in keeping with the thought of the times by its similarities to pseudo-Xenophon,[43] and we may confine ourselves to the first and third points. Pericles begins by saying that a city must stand together, since individual citizens, even if temporarily successful, will fail if the city as a whole fails and, conversely, will in the end succeed if the city succeeds (II 60.1–4). The thought is closely echoed by Erechtheus (fg. 360.16–26; cf. *Philoctetes* fg. 798), who, like Theseus in the *Suppliants*, seems to have worn the character of an ideal προστάτης; he concludes

εἴπερ γὰρ ἀριθμὸν οἶδα καὶ τοὐλάσσονος
τὸ μεῖζον, οὑνὸς οἶκος οὐ πλέον σθένει
πταίσας ἁπάσης πόλεος οὐδ' ἴσον φέρει.

The Periclean ideal is contrasted with the conduct of the

later demagogues (II 60.6, 65; VI 15), which, as was observed above,[44] Euripides criticizes in terms similar to the
historian's (*Suppl.* 232–37). After stating the folly of unnecessary war in much the same way as in *Troiades* 400,
Pericles goes on to say that, unlike the rest of the citizens,
he has not changed his original view that this war is
necessary (II 61.1–2). That consistency, aped by Cleon
(III 38.1), is commended by Erechtheus with other political
advice to his son, when he says (fg. 362.9–10; cf. Soph. *O.T.*
557),

δυοῖν παρόντοιν πραγμάτοιν πρὸς θάτερον
γνώμην προσάπτων τὴν ἐναντίαν μέθες.

And although, like Theseus (*Her.* 1226–28), Pericles admits
the power of unexpected reverses to bring men low, like
him again (1248–50), he encourages the citizens to resist
in a manner worthy of themselves (II 61.3–4). There
follows the passage on the naval power of Athens (II 62.1–3),
after which in a phrase which recalls the verbal distinctions
of Prodicus,[45] he urges the Athenians not merely to
φρόνημα but to καταφρόνημα. The words convey Pericles'
characteristic intellectuality, and contrasted as they are
with the far more usual statements on the unreliability of
hope (IV 108.4; *Hcld.* 169–70), give evidence of genuineness.

We come now to Pericles' celebrated apology for empire
(II 63), which to him is in essence an expression of men's
will to do (ὁ δρᾶν τι ... βουλόμενος II 64.4). Empire in-
volves labor, is dangerous to undertake, still more dangerous
to abandon, and contrasts wholly with that gentlemanly
quietude which will not recognize the harsh fact of power.

[44] Page 23.
[45] Cf. I 69.6; III 39.2, 72.1, 82.4. Cf. H. Mayer, *Prodikos von Keos* (Paderborn
1913) 48–54, who lists perhaps an excessive number of synonyms in Euripides,
omitting, however, what is possibly an early example, *Alc.* 727–28, also *Her.*
165–66.

Pericles, it may be observed, does not use the invidious word πολυπραγμοσύνη of the attitude which he describes, although the Athenian Euphemus does not scruple to do so at Camarina (VI 87.3). Its opposite is repeatedly called ἡσυχία or ἀπραγμοσύνη (II 63, 64.4; cf. I 70.8, II 40.2, VI 18.2) or, in a more flattering although not less oligarchic sense, σωφροσύνη (I 32.4, 84.2; III 82.8). W. Nestle[46] discussed the significance of these words as they touch Socrates' manner of life, and from a more historical point of view, H. T. Wade-Gery[47] saw in the present passage a reflection of the quarrel between the advocates of a small (and conservative) and an imperial (and democratic) Athens. But while the latter's view is quite justified since Pericles is in fact opposing the wealthy advocates of peace and conciliation, and since such a party was doubtless equally active in the early political struggles to which Wade-Gery applies the passage, still the contrast between ἀπραγμοσύνη and πολυπραγμοσύνη has a wider, more international significance, as the parallels of the *Suppliants* show. The ideas receive great emphasis there. When Aethra first urges Theseus to intervene in Thebes on behalf of the fallen Argives, she says that Athens is mocked by her foes for taking upon herself such foreign quarrels, yet proudly opposes them;

> ἐν γὰρ τοῖς πόνοισιν αὔξεται.
> αἱ δ' ἥσυχοι σκοτεινὰ πράσσουσαι πόλεις
> σκοτεινὰ καὶ βλέπουσιν εὐλαβούμεναι
>
> (*Suppl.* 323–25).

Pericles speaks in the same way of πόνοι in the present passage, and Alcibiades repeats the argument in the debate on intervention in Sicily (VI 18.2). The ideas recur at the

---

[46] "'Απραγμοσύνη," *Philologus* 81 (1925) 129–40.
[47] "Thucydides the Son of Melesias," *JHS* 52 (1932) 205–27, esp. 224–25.

culmination of the quarrel between Theseus and the Theban Herald (576–77):

Κη. πράσσειν σὺ πόλλ' εἴωθας ἥ τε σὴ πόλις.
Θη. τοιγὰρ πονοῦσα πολλὰ πόλλ' εὐδαιμονεῖ,

and it is significant that while Theseus is prepared to defend the unwritten laws, the Theban's whole argument is for acceptance and quietude at all cost (476–509). Now, as was said above, Euripides sees idealism in alliances where Thucydides sees policy alone; with that exception, the ideas of labor, of discontent with the status quo, and of consequent power and fame are the same in both authors. Basically, the contrast between πολυπραγμοσύνη and ἀπραγμοσύνη seems to describe the conflict between a rising and an established power. The Spartans, hereditary leaders of Greece, quite naturally deprecated change, and the established classes in any given city held the same views for the same reasons. Athens, on the other hand, conscious of her energy, alleged it as a justification of her empire, an empire which meant a shift of power, internationally, from Sparta to herself and, domestically, from the rich to the poor. To Athenians, then, the word πολυπραγμοσύνη, vulgar as its connotations could be to aristocrats, had nobler meanings; it was, in fact, as the correspondences between Thucydides and Euripides show, one of the watchwords which justified her rise from a second-class to a dominating power.

The concluding paragraph of Pericles' speech is echoed by Euripides in several minor ways: the exhortation to bear τὰ δαιμόνια (II 64.2; *Her.* 1228, *Phoe.* 382); the reminder that all things great decline (II 64.3; *Bellerophon* fg. 304, *Ino* fg. 415); the statement that it is worth enduring φθόνος for great ends (II 64.5; *Phoenix* fg. 814). Yet even these parallels, some of them from early plays, are significant in a speech the texture of which comports well with our earliest sources of Athenian political thought.

It has already been noted that Euripides speaks of the persuasiveness of an honest man's ἀξίωμα and arraigns the destructive self-interest of lesser politicians in much the same way as Thucydides in II 65. I therefore merely note a few further parallels to the latter idea (*Hcld.* 3–5, *Hec.* 254–57, *Her.* 588–92, *I.A.* 527, 1362), before passing to the debate between Cleon and Diodotus in the third book. In general cast, Cleon's speech reveals his characteristic reliance on διαβολή (III 38.2–3, 42–43; V 16.1; *Suppl.* 415–16; Aristoph. *Ach.* 380, 502, *Eq.* 710); in substance, its most striking part is a violent criticism of the ineffectiveness of democracy. Whereas Pericles had set forth the ἀρετή of the Athenians as a force mitigating the harshness of empire (II 40.4–5; cf. I 76.3–4), Cleon expounds the naked fact of power, the maintenance of which, he says, permits no feelings of οἶκτος or ἐπιείκεια (III 37.2, 40.2–3). Just so, Creon in the *Medea* asserts that pity is hostile to self-interest (349, 1051–52); indeed, few ideas recur more insistently in Euripides or seem to have troubled him more than that education, with all it implies of decency, pity, and fellow feeling, nevertheless can harm its possessor (*Med.* 291–305, *Hcld.* 458, *Hipp.* 955–57, *Her.* 299–301, *Elec.* 294–96). And it is exactly this softening influence of the mind that Cleon attacks. He therefore repudiates Pericles' ideal of intelligent debate, asserting οἵ τε φαυλότεροι τῶν ἀνθρώπων πρὸς τοὺς ξυνετωτέρους ὡς ἐπὶ τὸ πλέον ἄμεινον οἰκοῦσι τὰς πόλεις (III 37.3), to which one may compare the lines of the nearly contemporary *Andromache* (481–82),

> σοφῶν τε πλῆθος ἀθρόον ἀσθενέστερον
> φαυλοτέρας φρενὸς αὐτοκρατοῦς.

Such criticism of the divided leadership of democracy is

Three Essays on Thucydides

inevitable always and never more so than in wartime, although Pericles had so avoided it that the historian saw in his ascendancy the rule of one man (II 65.10). The misfortune is, as Thucydides means to show, that to escape it one must return, as Cleon in fact does, to a harsh travesty of the Spartan ideal (cf. the present passage to I 84.3 and III 83.3).

Cleon goes on to attack not merely softness of feeling, but delight in words (III 38.3–7). One may compare Phaedra's remarks on the influences hostile to reason (*Hipp.* 383–85),

εἰσὶ δ' ἡδοναὶ πολλαὶ βίου,
μακραί τε λέσχαι καὶ σχολή, τερπνόν κακόν,
αἰδώς τε,

as well as the Nurse's characterization of the queen's sick mood (*Hipp.* 184–85),

οὐδέ σ' ἀρέσκει τὸ παρόν, τὸ δ' ἀπὸν
φίλτερον ἡγῇ,

to Cleon's similar indictment of the Athenian temper (III 38.7), ζητοῦντές τε ἄλλο τι ὡς εἰπεῖν ἢ ἐν οἷς ζῶμεν (cf. also *Alc.* 202–3). The contexts here are quite different, but the essential similarity of expression shows at least that Cleon is using the language of his time. And the same is true when he sees in the previous good fortune of the Mytileneans the cause of their rebellion and draws from it the old moral, often repeated in Euripides (cf. *Suppl.* 124), that most men cannot bear prosperity (III 39.4). But finally, one should not leave Cleon's speech without noting its general similarity to several well-known speeches of tragedy. In the *Antigone* when the attempted burial of Polynices has been revealed, Creon shows his innate violence by immediately alleging disloyalty and profit as

30

Euripides and Thucydides

motives of the crime and by descanting on these at length and in the most general terms (*Antig.* 280–301; cf. *O.T.* 125, 380). The same rash intensity showing itself in sweeping accusations appears in the speeches of Theseus in the *Hippolytus* (936–80), Pentheus in the *Bacchae* (215–62), and Jason in the *Medea* (446–64). The opening words of the last speech,

οὐ νῦν κατεῖδον πρῶτον ἀλλὰ πολλάκις,

surprisingly resemble Cleon's, πολλάκις μὲν ἤδη ἔγωγε καὶ ἄλλοτε ἔγνων δημοκρατίαν (III 37.1). It is notable too that, just as the foregoing speeches of tragedy are followed by careful and logical replies—one thinks especially of Hippolytus' extremely careful self-defense (*Hipp.* 983–1035; cf. Soph. *O.T.* 577–615)—so the following speech of Diodotus is remarkable for compressed and tightly woven argument. Now it seems beyond question that Euripides and Thucydides are consciously attempting the same contrast of impetuosity and reason, and it might therefore be argued that the historian is here adopting the methods of tragedy. Another explanation, not wholly incompatible with the first, is that both authors are portraying a well-known type of speech which in its violence neglected the ordinary rules of rhetoric and relied on the forceful outpouring of familiar judgments. Thucydides, at least, calls Cleon βιαιότατος τῶν πολιτῶν (III 36.6), and Aristotle (*Ath. Pol.* 28.15) says of him, πρῶτος ἐπὶ τοῦ βήματος ἀνέκραγε καὶ ἐλοιδορήσατο... τῶν ἄλλων ἐν κόσμῳ λεγόντων. If the second explanation be accepted, then it follows once more that Thucydides is true to the period when he distinguishes between orderly and disorderly forms of argument. For Euripides, as we have seen, makes that distinction in plays as early as the *Medea* and the *Hippolytus*.

The orderliness of Diodotus' reply shows itself at the start in his neat and balanced clauses. In a manner similar to *Orestes* 490 and *Archelaus* fg. 257, he begins by noting factors that impede sound judgment (III 42.1), and goes on to observe that those who oppose debate are either unintelligent or venal, a form of antithesis to which one may compare *Heracles* 347 (cf. Soph. *O.T.* 535),

ἀμαθής τις εἶ θεός, ἢ δίκαιος οὐκ ἔφυς.

Then after dwelling at some length on the harm resulting from διαβολή, he turns to the burden of his speech, namely, that the subject cities are to be tended for profit, not judged by abstract right (III 44)—a forceful use of the argument from τὸ συμφέρον. When, to support his views, he adduces men's proneness to act on their desires in spite of all deterrents (III 45), he touches perhaps the central idea of both the *Medea* and the *Hippolytus*, the heroines of which state that they know their error but are irresistibly drawn to follow it (*Med.* 1078–80, *Hipp.* 373–87; cf. *Andr.* 368–69, *I.T.* 414). It is interesting that Diodotus expounds an evolutionary view of law, confirming it, like Thucydides in the Archaeology, by an allusion to Homer (III 45.3); and from the speech of Protagoras in Plato (*Protag.* 320d–322), the Hippocratic Περὶ Ἀρχαίης Ἰητρικῆς, and the interest of all the tragedians in the development of society,[48] his words seem entirely natural. He ends by elaborating the statement of the *Medea* (290–91) that prevention is better than cure (III 46.4) and by saying that, even if the subject cities do revolt, Athens should pretend not to see (III 47.4)—advice frequently given in Euripides (*Ino* fg. 413, *Hipp.* 462–66, *I.T.* 956). Finally, to say a word of the speech as a whole, it is noteworthy that Diodotus opposes Cleon's position of

[48] Aesch. *Prom.* 442–506, fg. 182; Soph. *Antig.* 332–76, fg. 479 (Pearson); Eur. *Suppl.* 201–13, *Elec.* 743–45, fg. 578; Critias *Sisyphus* fg. 1.

rigid justice with the same cool arguments from the laws of nature and from personal profit with which the Nurse in the *Hippolytus* (433–81, 500–502) disputes Phaedra's more idealistic stand. This practice of refuting τὸ δίκαιον by τὸ συμφέρον seems to have been well known,[49] and the debate between Phaedra and the Nurse makes it quite certain that such tactics were familiar in the Athens of Cleon and Diodotus.

Since I have dwelt with perhaps excessive detail on the foregoing speeches, a simple summary of parallels should in most cases suffice henceforth, and of the Plataean speech[50] I merely observe that, like *Medea* 475–95 and *Orestes* 640–79, it rests on a recitation of past benefits (III 54.2–56) and, like *Suppliants* 297–319, on an appeal to the Spartans not to disgrace their name or the religious laws of Greece (III 57–58)

The historian's brilliant catalogue later in the same book (III 82–83) of the effects of war on the public mind does not, for obvious reasons, resemble anything in tragedy, but Euripides parallels a few of its expressions and ideas, and its general form is perhaps not inexplicable in the light of fifth-century thought. To discuss the parallels first, Euripides speaks of war as meaning the abandonment of the εὐσέβεια common in peace (III 82.2; *Ion* 1045–47), of poverty as teaching men evil (III 82.7; *Elec.* 376; cf. ps.-Xen. *Ath. Pol.* 1.6), of the poor as therefore inclined to impute evil motives (III 83.1; *I.T.* 678), and of the distortion of standards in times of excitement (III 82.4; *Hec.* 607–8),

[49] In *Hec.* 251–331, the aged queen appeals to Odysseus to save the life of Polyxena, asserting (271), τῷ μὲν δικαίῳ τόνδ' ἀμιλλῶμαι λόγον. He replies (315–16) that giving honors to the dead conduces to valor. Similarly Jason refutes Medea's just plea on grounds of practicality (*Med.* 559–67). Cf. also *Bacch.* 334–36.

[50] With the Plataeans' conciliatory opening in which they speak of their sad plight and their fear (III 53), compare the early fragments *Alcmeon in Psophis* fg. 67 and *Telephus* fg. 703, also Aristophanes' judgment of Euripides as a master of appeal (*Ach.* 415–18). See also C. T. Murphy, "Aristophanes and the Art of Rhetoric," *HSCP* 49 (1938) 88–92.

Three Essays on Thucydides

ἀκόλαστος ὄχλος ναυτική τ' ἀναρχία
κρείσσων πυρός, κακὸς δ' ὁ μή τι δρῶν κακόν.

The idea, in fact, that misfortune can in itself do much to vitiate men's natures had a strong grip on the thought of the fifth century from the time of Simonides on,[51] and although Sophocles especially expounded the nobler faith that a naturally good man somehow keeps true to himself through disaster, it was characteristic of Euripides that he felt the former more mechanistic view profoundly. Now it is not a great step from grasping that truth and applying it in individual characters as Euripides does, for instance, in the *Hecuba* and *Electra*, to applying it in social terms like Thucydides. Such statements as that of Euphemus (VI 85.1), ἀνδρὶ δὲ τυράννῳ ἢ πόλει ἀρχὴν ἐχούσῃ οὐδὲν ἄλογον ὅτι ξυμφέρον, and *Hecuba* 903–4,

ἰδίᾳ θ' ἑκάστῳ καὶ πόλει, τὸν μὲν κακὸν
κακόν τι πάσχειν, τὸν δὲ χρηστὸν εὐτυχεῖν,

are examples of the pervasive Greek habit of seeing the same truths embodied in the individual and in the mass. And although one touches here on profound questions concerning the nature of Greek thought and art, it can at least be said that Thucydides' desire to see the typical is not unique in him. On the contrary, the whole rhetorical doctrine of εἰκός depended on the conception that different ages and conditions of men would act consistently and hence predictably. The Old Oligarch sketches what is typical in the action of the κακοί with no less broad strokes than does Hippolytus the probable conduct of an upright young man (*Hipp.* 983–1020). Both argue the particular case by observations on the type. Or again, when Medea urges the chorus

---

[51] E. Diehl, *Anthologia Lyrica Graeca* (Leipzig 1925) fg. 4.10–11, πρᾶξας γὰρ εὖ πᾶς ἀνὴρ ἀγαθός, | κακὸς δ' εἰ κακῶς. Cf. Soph. *Antig.* 564–65. *Elec.* 617–20; Eur. *I.T.* 351–53.

to silence, she speaks at length of the general lot of women (*Med.* 230–51), and when she pleads with Creon, she adduces the suspicion always accorded the wise (*Med.* 292–301). In short, one need hardly multiply examples to show that Euripides thought of rhetoric as adducing fundamental laws of human nature and society to prove, as the case might be, what was δίκαιον or συμφέρον or εἰκός.[52] It follows that Thucydides, reared in a similar rhetoric, expected and was doubtless trained to see the general law underlying the specific occurrence, and although his greatness as an historian depends also on his wide personal experience and his unique care in verifying facts, yet his *History* would lack its essence without such searching generalizations as those of the present passage. There is no question here, as in the speeches, of authenticity; the parallels adduced from Euripides show rather the prevailing breadth of the rhetoric with which Thucydides approached both his speeches and his *History* itself.

The fourth book calls for little comment beside that given in passing hitherto. The speech of the Spartans, seeking

[52] So Aristotle, *Rhet.* I 2.7 (1356a28), says that rhetoric is παραφυές τι τῆς διαλεκτικῆς ... καὶ τῆς περὶ τὰ ἤθη πραγματείας, ἣν δίκαιόν ἐστι προσαγορεύειν πολιτικήν. He repeatedly says that to discuss any given subject demands a familiarity with the general principles involved (cf. I 4.8, 1359b36; 4.9, 1360a3). For rhetoric deals with what is probably true of the class, rather than of the individual (I 2.11, 1356b34). Thus in describing τὸ συμβουλευτικόν, he first discusses the nature of happiness (I 5), then of what conduces to happiness (I 6), and finally the kinds of polities under which men live (I 8; cf. I 8.1, 1365b23, μέγιστον δὲ καὶ κυριώτατον ἁπάντων πρὸς τὸ δύνασθαι πείθειν καὶ καλῶς συμβουλεύειν, τὰς πολιτείας ἁπάσας λαβεῖν καὶ τὰ ἑκάστης ἔθη καὶ νόμιμα καὶ συμφέροντα διελεῖν). He expounds the underlying principles of epideictic and dicanic oratory with similar breadth (I 9.1–13 and I 11–12). In short, he conceived of rhetoric as utilizing the general truths derived from the more specialized studies of ethics, psychology, and government. Even the *Rhet. ad Alex.*, superficial as it is, describes the nature of democracy and oligarchy (1424a8–1424b16) in treating τὸ συμβουλευτικόν. And although it is true that government and ethics were not studied in the fifth century with that specialism which they received in the fourth, they were all the more associated with rhetoric at the beginning. So Protagoras is represented by Plato (*Protag.* 318e5) as teaching εὐβουλία περὶ τῶν οἰκείων ... καὶ περὶ τῶν τῆς πόλεως, ὅπως τὰ τῆς πόλεως δυνατώτατος ἂν εἴη καὶ πράττειν καὶ λέγειν, instruction which Socrates (319a3) characterizes as τὴν πολιτικὴν τέχνην. Cf. above, n. 33.

peace at Athens while their countrymen were surrounded on Sphacteria, is however interesting as beginning with an apology for their speaking at some length, which they say Spartans do not ordinarily do but can if necessary (IV 17.2). So, Euripides, seemingly to avoid incongruity, makes Cassandra say that she can argue rationally, wild as were her earlier utterances (*Tro.* 366–67). The parallel suggests that Thucydides feels some inappropriateness in attributing to Spartans the rhetoric which, I have argued, was common in the Athens which he knew. The question is difficult. It has usually been assumed that Thucydides unhesitatingly imposed his own style on all his speakers, but our evidence on the point is not clear. For although Herodotus seems to keep a uniform style in his speeches, Aeschylus and Sophocles varied theirs, especially for humble characters, while Aristophanes introduces dialect, and Plato in the *Symposium*, for instance, conspicuously mimics his speakers. Thucydides himself attributes terseness to the ephor Sthenelaidas, elevation to Pericles, and violence to Cleon; he evidently tries to impart, if not a speaker's cast of language, as least the sequence and quality of his thought. All that has been said hitherto goes to show that he is faithful in the case of Athenian speakers, but the present parallel may indicate that he consciously gave up the attempt in reporting foreigners, especially Spartans. Further parallels in Euripides to the speech of the Spartans are the appeal to quiet reason (IV 17.3; *Suppl.* 476–78), the statement that victors should not trust their luck too far (IV 18.3; *Hec.* 282–83),[53] that good luck gives good repute (IV 18.5; *Hcld.* 745–47), that conciliation is possible through noblesse (IV 19.2–3; *Her.* 299–301).

[53] Cf. *Rhet. ad Alex.* 1425a38, ἤδη δ' ἐνεστῶτα [πόλεμον] παύειν ἐπιχειροῦντας ... τοῦτο πρῶτον λεκτέον, ὅτι δεῖ τοὺς νοῦν ἔχοντας μὴ περιμένειν ἕως ἂν πέσωσιν.

The events following Delium, described near the end of
the fourth book, are likewise interesting in their connection
with the *Suppliants*, which reflects the peculiar bitterness felt
between the two neighboring cities after the battle. Thucydides, who indirectly reports the speeches on both sides,
makes clear that each had grievances: the Athenians because
their dead were not returned, the Thebans because Athens
had fortified the precinct of Apollo at Delium (IV 97–98).
The argument, as in the *Suppliants*, turns on τὰ νόμιμα τῶν
Ἑλλήνων (IV 97.2, 98.2; *Suppl.* 122–23, 311, 526, 563), but
in the fiction of Euripides Theseus does what in fact the
Thebans taunted Athens with being unable to do, namely,
to retrieve and bury the dead (IV 99; *Suppl.* 571). The
Athenians, for their part, justified their occupation as a
necessary act, forgivable in the eyes of the god (IV 98.6), a
plea used by Euripides (*Hipp. Kal.* fg. 433, *I.A.* 394–95),
although not in the *Suppliants* where Athens is faultless.

But the play, which did not immediately follow Delium,
refers also to events described early in the fifth book if, as
seems the case,[54] the oath prescribed by Athena (1191–93),

> μήποτ' Ἀργείους χθόνα
> ἐς τήνδ' ἐποίσειν πολέμιον παντευχίαν,
> ἄλλων τ' ἰόντων ἐμποδὼν θήσειν δόρυ,

gives a one-sided version of the treaty (V 47; *IG* I² 86)
between Athens, Argos, Mantinea, and Elis, which makes
in effect the same prescription (V 47.2–4). But if this point
is more significant for Euripides than Thucydides, the
opposite is true of the references, already noted, to the
duplicity of Sparta (*Suppl.* 187) and the self-interest of

---

[54] Absolute certainty is impossible, since a clause of mutual defense was perhaps
already a commonplace in treaties, as it later became (*IG* II² 1, 14 and 15). Thus
Euripides may possibly have in mind the general usage rather than the specific
pact of 420 (cf. above, n. 15).

the younger politicians (232–37).[55] For, in describing the events immediately following the Peace of Nicias the historian makes exactly the latter point of Alcibiades (V 43.2, and more fully in VI 15.2–3), noting his youth, φιλονικία, need of money, and desire for adventurous policy, in language often very close to the more general sketch of Euripides. The duplicity of Sparta, a familiar criticism uttered in the earlier *Andromache*, was especially felt in Athens at this time because of Sparta's tortuous policy in encouraging Thebes while still bound by the terms of the Peace (V 36–38, 40–43).When, therefore, Thucydides recurs to the idea both in speech and in narrative (V 36.1, 39.2, 42.2, 43.3, 45.3), and at the same time expounds the weakness of Alcibiades, he is demonstrably echoing the very thoughts of the period.

The *Trojan Women* and the Melian Dialogue have superficially little in common; for although they share, I think, the same essential attitude toward the event, the one elaborates the emotions suggested by it, while the other sets forth the policies which were its cause. To Thucydides' mind the siege seems to have been culpable in two ways: first, as a departure, foreshadowing greater departures, from Pericles' plan of war (I 65.7),[56] and second, as a symbol of the increasing brutalization of the Greek mind (III 82.3), a brutalization which he traces from Pericles' ideal of ἀρετή towards the subject cities (II 40.4), through Cleon's doctrine of naked power, to the present passage, and which he like-

---

[55] It is no objection that Euripides makes these criticisms of the heroes who attacked Thebes, rather than of Athenians. He is not arguing a case but expressing ideas which are in the air, as is clear not only from his references to Delium and Sparta but from the pronouncements in favor of peace (134–49, 950–55).

[56] At the start of the war Melos was outside the Delian Confederacy (II 9.4). Athens tried unsuccessfully to reduce the island in 426 (III 91.1), and in the following year imposed a tribute of fifteen talents (*IG* I² 63, line 65), whether paid or not, we do not know. Thus the conquest of the island represents the very kind of extension of Athenian naval power which Pericles had feared even to suggest (II 62.1).

wise observes in the intensified rivalry of the demagogues. If this interpretation is correct, then the Dialogue embodies the same attitude as is openly expressed in the prologue of the *Trojan Women* (esp. 95–97), namely, that disaster awaits the victors. But although so much might be granted and although the two works contain other similarities to be noted below, it is not primarily by such means that Thucydides' veracity can be defended. Rather it must first be shown that the method of dialogue was in fact so familiar at the time that the Athenians and Melians might actually have used it in some such way as Thucydides reports them to have done. Now that presumption is not hard to establish and, for want of it, the historian's accuracy has too often been impugned. In the passage of the *Soph. Elench.* (34.183b36) already cited, Aristotle says of Gorgias and other sophists that λόγους οἱ μὲν ῥητορικούς, οἱ δὲ ἐρωτη-τικοὺς ἐδίδοσαν ἐκμανθάνειν, and the so-called Δισσοὶ Λόγοι (*Vorsokr.*[9] II 405–16), which derive from some non-Attic source about the year 400, show exactly such arguments for use in dialogue. But the practice went back to the middle of the century, when Zeno and Melissus entrapped their philosophic opponents by question and answer, and when Protagoras, if he was the first to do so, took the important step of adapting the method to political discussion.[57] Plato's *Euthydemus*, the dramatic date of which seems to be before 415,[58] speaks of the brothers Euthydemus and Dionysodorus as having long carried on their eristic trade in many parts of the Greek world (271c), and it is quite evident that Socrates was unique in practicing, not dialogue, but only dialogue. For at least the more celebrated sophists claimed equal skill in question and answer and in

[57] See above, n. 33.
[58] A. E. Taylor, *Plato, The Man and His Work*[3] (London 1929) 90.

continuous speaking, and although their pupils doubtless had more use for the latter and practiced it more as Plato says they did (*Protag.* 329a), still they could not have been ignorant of the former. Now the reason why Socrates preferred dialogue was that it permitted more careful thought, and it is significant that the Athenians at Melos advance exactly this reason for conferring privately rather than speaking in the assembly. When they reject the latter course, ὅπως δὴ μὴ ξυνεχεῖ ῥήσει οἱ πολλοὶ ἐπαγωγὰ καὶ ἀνέλεγκτα εἰσάπαξ ἀκούσαντες ἡμῶν ἀπατηθῶσιν (V 85), they make the same points against oratory that are made in the *Protagoras* (329a–b, 336c–d), namely, that it is attractive but misleading because it obscures logic and is heard only once. In sum, Protagoras' early reputation in the art and the clear proofs that it was widely practiced, being considered more suitable than oratory for close reasoning, confirm the essential good faith of Thucydides. It cannot have seemed surprising to him, and need not to us, that Athenian generals should have argued step by step with the magistrates of Melos the issues of submission or resistance.

The actual parallels to the Melian Dialogue in Euripides are fairly numerous. The Athenians begin by limiting discussion to the question of advantage (V 89–99), a topic familiar in the *Medea*,[59] and when the Melians reply that they would be disgraced by not resisting (V 100), rejoin, like the kindlier Talthybius (*Tro.* 728), that the weak must not pretend to what befits the strong. Like the Trojan women, they are commanded to think simply of saving life itself (V 93; *Tro.* 729–39). When then they urge the uncertainty of the future, the Athenians crush them (V 103) with the same figure from risking all on one throw and the same reminder of the futility of mere hope that are expressed

[59] See above, p. 12.

in a similar situation by the Argive Herald in the *Heraclidae* (148–49, 169–70; cf. *Her.* 91–94, 282–83, 309–10). The Melians now advance their trust both in the gods, who, they say, will protect their righteous cause (V 104), and in Sparta. Their stand recalls the bitter lines of the *Bellerophon* (fg. 286.10–12),

πόλεις τε μικρὰς οἶδα τιμώσας θεούς,
αἳ μειζόνων κλύουσι δυσσεβεστέρων
λόγχης ἀριθμῷ πλείονος κρατούμεναι.

When the Athenians reply that, in acting according to the laws of nature, they themselves are not offending the gods who presumably submit to the same laws (V 105.1–2), the thought is close to Hecuba's in the familiar line (*Tro.* 886),

Ζεύς, εἴτ' ἀνάγκη φύσεος εἴτε νοῦς βροτῶν.

The passage in which they go on to remind the Melians how empty is any trust in the supremely politic Spartans (V 105.4–109) has been mentioned above.[60] Just so, the Spartan Menelaus in the *Orestes* (718–24) is portrayed as quite capable of deserting the ties of blood when it is dangerous to defend them. The sentence in which the Athenians praise their opponents' innocence but deplore their folly (V 105.3) recalls the line of the *Alcestis* (1093),

αἰνῶ μὲν αἰνῶ· μωρίαν δ' ὀφλισκάνεις.

The whole attitude of the Melians is aptly summarized in the words of Talthybius (*Tro.* 302–3),

κάρτα τοι τοὐλεύθερον
ἐν τοῖς τοιούτοις δυσλόφως φέρει κακά.

Finally to speak of the debate as a whole, it expounds more openly than any other part of Thucydides' work those

[60] Page 19.

principles of power which, from the Archaeology on, play a profound part in his thought, but which, nevertheless, if we may judge by his admiration of Pericles who insisted that ἀρετή must accompany power, were not to him the sole law of empire. Now Thucydides was not the only Athenian to ponder these questions; on the contrary, the rival claims of generosity and self-interest, familiar in the *Medea*, are discussed in the papyrus fragment of Antiphon's Ἀλήθεια[61] and form perhaps the central issue in the whole complex controversy of φύσις and νόμος which Plato represents as going back to this period (*Gorg.* 482c–486c; *Rep.* 338c). It can then be accepted that there were men in Athens who, like Callicles in the *Gorgias*, believed exclusively in the doctrine of power; Eteocles in the *Phoenissae* (503–6, 524–25) is, for instance, portrayed as such a man. Hence there exist no general grounds for doubting Thucydides' view that in 416 the directors of Athenian policy in fact held such ideas in regard to the empire. If, further, the previous point be granted, that the arts not merely of oratory but of dialogue were taught by the sophists and practiced by their pupils, then we must believe that such an argument as the Melian Dialogue could actually have taken place. For although, like all Thucydides' speeches, it is compressed and therefore more abstract than an actual debate would have been, yet it closely touches the thought of the time, proceeds by arguments which are familiar in Euripides and hence in Athens, and relies, as we have seen that contemporary rhetoric did rely, on general propositions to support specific proposals.

I shall say little of books six and seven, both because the main lines of comparison between Thucydides and Euripides have already been sketched and because the speeches in

[61] *Vorsokr.*[9] II 346–55, fg. 44.

these books contain in fact far fewer parallels to the latter. It is true that, like the speeches of earlier books, they commonly rely on arguments from the profitable, the just, or the likely, and to that extent reveal principles of rhetoric familiar in Euripides. But he can hardly be expected to touch on the actual issues which arose in Sicily, and it is instructive that such parallels as exist in his plays are chiefly to the speeches made in Athens before the expedition and to the letter and speeches of Nicias, who once, at least, under the stress of danger repeated familiar ideas (VII 69.2). The argument from silence may then be of value here; for if it is true, as I think it is, that Thucydides is closest to Euripides when he sets forth what either took place at Athens or could have been directly reported there, in some cases before his own exile, then his accuracy is the more authenticated. Conversely, the common assumption that he was in Sicily and got his information on events there from local sources will likewise be confirmed.

Perhaps the chief resemblance in Euripides to the debate before the expedition lies in the conflict of interests, drawn there, between old and young (VI 12.2–13; 18.6). In the *Suppliants*, as we have seen, it is the young leaders who mislead the state for their own interests (νέοις παραχθείς, 232). The mss. likewise give νέων in *Heracles* 257 as the revolutionary followers of Lycus (cf. 588–92), and the reading, although not above question, seems confirmed by the general opposition of the aged chorus to their new rulers. And if in both these passages, young leaders are portrayed as the ruin of other cities than Athens, in the *Erechtheus* (fg. 362.21) the old king, among much advice tending to the same end, bids his son

ὁμιλίας δὲ τὰς γεραιτέρων φίλει.

Now a sense of conflict between the generations is already apparent in the *Acharnians* (esp. 702–18) and, as the parallels in Euripides show, continued in men's minds through the years shortly before and after the Peace of Nicias. It was undoubtedly connected with the policies of Alcibiades and his followers, and hence can only be expected to have flamed out with open violence in the critical debates on Sicily. Of the further parallels between the poet and the historian in the latter's estimate of Alcibiades (VI 15) enough has been said above; so also in regard to the πολυπραγμοσύνη of Athens, talked of in this book both by the latter (VI 18) and by Euphemus (VI 87.2–3). Two remaining points might perhaps be mentioned. When Nicias (VI 13.2) urges that Egesta be left to get out of the difficulties which she had entered of her own accord, he echoes the counsel of Theseus in the *Suppliants* (248–49) before the latter decides to intervene in Thebes on religious grounds. And Alcibiades' forecast that the democracy of Syracuse could never unite or offer effective resistance (VI 17.2–6)—a forecast disproved in the event and, although not to Thucydides' mind the primary cause of the defeat (II 65), still an important factor in it (VII 55.2, VIII 96.5)— seems not to have been shared by Euripides. At least in the *Trojan Women* (220–23) he goes out of his way to praise the valor of the land of Aetna, a view which corresponds to Nicias' estimate of the approaching task (VI 20.4), and which therefore indirectly confirms the whole substance of the debate.

The resemblances in the seventh book, with one exception to be noted below, are closest in the letter and speeches of Nicias. He wrote to the Athenians, Thucydides says (VII 8.2), because he feared the falsification of messengers, a point made in the *Heraclidae* (292–93). And when in the

letter itself he concludes his account of the army by re-
marking on the difficulty which he has in maintaining
discipline, he makes a complaint which must have been
all too familiar at Athens and which in one form or another
appears several times in Euripides (*Hcld.* 415–24, *Hec.*
606–8, 855–61, *Suppl.* 247, *I.A.* 914). His remark that he is
sending unpleasant but necessary information (VII 14.4)
recalls the very similar words of Orestes (*Elec.* 293), likewise for use in a message. In Nicias' exhortation before the
great final battle in the harbor, there is little to be noted for
our purpose except his reminder to the sailors what benefits
they had enjoyed by living in Athens and being thought
Athenians (VII 63.3). One thinks of Jason recalling to Medea
the similar benefits which she had had from Greece (*Med.*
536–41), doubly immoral words on his part, since such
reminders must have been the common substance of more
worthy appeals. But when the fight was near, Thucydides
says, Nicias forgot formal reasoning and resorted to such
old and natural pleas as Aeschylus tells were uttered at
Salamis—pleas to wife, children, and ancestral gods (VII
69.2; *Pers.* 403–5; cf. *Septem* 14–16, Eur. *Erech.* fg. 360.15).
The passage is interesting; for it shows, what has been
argued from the beginning, that Thucydides thought of
the Athenians as so accustomed to polished and logical
argument that only under the stress of extreme emotion
would they lose their fear of that trite but universal elo-
quence, ἀρχαιολογεῖν, which had been used unashamedly a
half century before. When at last the army was in retreat,
Nicias sought to encourage the soldiers by recalling to
them the ancient doctrine of expiation, saying that they had
suffered enough for past errors and good fortune was in
store (VII 77.1–4). It is not hard to imagine that he both
believed and could have expressed these ideas, which in the

plays of Euripides rise naturally to men's lips in time of danger (*Her.* 101–6, *I.T.* 721–22, *Hel.* 1082, 1446–50).

Finally, when Thucydides says of Nicias after his death that he least deserved such a fate because his whole life had been governed by principles of virtue (VII 86.5), he echoes what seems to have been the judgment of Euripides, who at the end of the *Electra* (1351–52) sends the Dioscuri off to Sicily to help the righteous—

οἷσιν δ' ὅσιον καὶ τὸ δίκαιον
φίλον ἐν βιότῳ.

The same judgment seemingly underlies the portrait of Capaneus (*Suppl.* 861–71), which in its broad lines is apparently sketched from Nicias.[62] Thucydides' words have been wrongly suspected of a double meaning. For, although to his mind Nicias lacked qualities absolutely essential in a general and possessed by Pericles, namely, realism of outlook and the ability to control the people, still he did possess one vital attribute of the great statesman which all the other successors lacked, his uprightness. And the passages from Euripides show how profound an effect that one quality made on his contemporaries.

Since I shall say nothing of the eighth book, which lacks speeches, the review of parallel passages is now complete except in one respect, namely, the similarity between Thucydides' descriptions and the ῥήσεις of tragedy. For, although the subject deserves far more space than can be given it here, it is worthwhile, if only for the sake of completeness, to observe that in seeking Thucydides' possible models for such a description as that of the battle in the harbor of Syracuse, one is inevitably drawn to tragedy rather than to Herodotus. From an artistic point of view, it

[62] Cf. P. Giles, "Political Allusions in the *Supplices* of Euripides," *CR* 4 (1890) 95–98, and E. C. Marchant, *Thucydides, Book VII* (London 1919) xxxvii.

Euripides and Thucydides

would be hard to imagine a greater contrast than that
between the descriptions of Salamis by Aeschylus and by
Herodotus, and there can be little question that the account
of the battle of Syracuse has much in common with the
former and almost nothing with the latter. Herodotus,
although he signifies the broad divisions of time in the
battle (VIII 83.2, 89.2, 91), interrupts his account by telling
who opposed whom, what Xerxes is reported to have said,
what befell individual leaders on either side; his narrative
does not fall into clearly marked divisions, achieves no
suspense through the balance of part against part, and rises
to no climax. The opposite is true of the ῥῆσις of the *Persae*,
and one can note a marked similarity to it in the account of
the battle of Syracuse. Both describe with gathering emotion
the exhortations before the battle, the first successes of the
ultimately beaten (VII 70.2; *Pers.* 412), then the coupling of
ships in the narrows (VII 70.4; *Pers.* 413) and the supreme
agony of conflict, and finally the flight of the defeated with
outcry and groaning (VII 71.6, οἰμωγῇ τε καὶ στόνῳ; *Pers.*
426–27, οἰμωγὴ δ' ὁμοῦ | κωκύμασιν). Both see each stage
of the battle in relation to the whole; both pass with sure
steps from the gathering to the height of the action, then
to its decline and end. Their difference lies chiefly in the
historian's greater detail and in his deeper interest in the
feelings of combatants and spectators. And, significantly, it
is in much these same respects that Euripides too departs
from Aeschylus. Like Thucydides (VII 70.7), he observes
the cries in the height of an action (*Hcld.* 839–40, *Suppl.*
702, 711–12, *Phoen.* 1145); creates the simultaneous impression of many single struggles (VII 70.6; *Suppl.* 683–93)
and the sense of the noise and shifting fortunes of battle
(*Hcld.* 832–38); he even portrays the effects of the struggle
on observers (*Phoen.* 1388–89, *Suppl.* 719–20), as Thucydides

47

does at much greater length at the climax of his description (VII 71.1–4). In short, although Thucydides, having a definite event in mind, conveys a greater sense of reality than Euripides and is more copious and exact in details and, it need hardly be said, far more moving, yet his climactic order, his interest in men's feelings, and above all, his pervading tragic emotion betray a deep kinship with the developed ῥήσεις of drama. It has been said that Gorgias emulated in prose the charm of poetry.[63] Certainly it is as true to say that the tragedians, rather than Herodotus, taught both the means by which description must proceed and the heights to which it may aspire.

Finally, I have noted a few descriptive phrases in Euripides so similar to those of the historian as to call for special mention. Early in the *Phoenissae* (161–62), Electra looking from the walls at the besieging Argives says,

ὁρῶ δῆτ᾽ οὐ σαφῶς, ὁρῶ δέ πως
μορφῆς τύπωμα στέρνα τ᾽ ἐξῃκασμένα,

words which vividly recall the night battle on Epipolae (VII 44.2), when men saw ὡς ἐν σελήνῃ εἰκὸς τὴν μὲν ὄψιν τοῦ σώματος προορᾶν, τὴν δὲ γνῶσιν τοῦ οἰκείου ἀπιστεῖσθαι. And Euripides clearly alludes to the fighting at Syracuse when, later in the same play (727–28), Eteocles and Creon, canvassing methods of attack, speak first of the dangers of a sally at night and then of attacking while the enemy is at mess (cf. VII 40). As was noted above, Euripides also observes the effect of battle on the spectators: one may compare καὶ ἀπὸ τῶν δρωμένων τῆς ὄψεως καὶ τὴν γνώμην μᾶλλον τῶν ἐν τῷ ἔργῳ ἐδουλοῦντο (VII 71.3) to

πλείων δὲ τοῖς ὁρῶσιν ἐστάλασσ᾽ ἱδρὼς
ἢ τοῖσι δρῶσι, διὰ φίλων ὀρρωδίαν

(*Phoen.* 1388–89).

[63] Navarre (above, n. 9) 110.

Like the encircled Plataeans (III 20.3–4), Capaneus prepares for attack by calculating the height of the opposing walls (*Phoen.* 180–81), and Polynices entering Thebes alone feels the same terror of being surrounded by enemies (*Phoen.* 269–71) as, in the historian's account, the Thebans feel when they are first entrapped in Plataea (II 3.4). It is, in fact, remarkable how many phrases in this one play, the *Phoenissae*, recall Thucydides. Like the defenders of Epidaurus (V 55), Eteocles will not treat with an enemy under arms (*Phoen.* 510–12); like Pericles, Jocasta says one must bear the afflictions of heaven (II 64.2; *Phoen.* 382); like Nicias, Eteocles forgets under emotion the fear of triteness (VII 69.2; *Phoen.* 438). But in all these similarities there seems to be no question of direct borrowing. Since Thucydides was recounting what he had heard from witnesses, if any one was the borrower, it should be Euripides. And yet chronology seems to make that impossible. It follows that both men had in mind events and situations commonly known. But if so, one is driven again to the conclusion made in the last paragraph: that Thucydides often sought in prose the effects hitherto achieved only in verse, or to put it in another way, that verse for its part was so affected by the rise of rhetoric that Euripides and Thucydides both in speeches and in descriptions could often work by the same methods for the same ends.

III

It remains only to summarize the conclusions reached hitherto.

(1) Certain passages of Euripides touch upon the method and outlook of the *History*. The poet criticizes his own predecessors, questions their criteria, and in a broader sense

abandons their idealism for a more exact appraisal of life. Even, perhaps especially, the early plays and fragments show him fully conversant with such conflicts as those between decency and self-interest, right and power, word and motive, apparent and hidden cause. He can see character as molded by events and can look upon acts, usually called immoral, as the results of profound natural impulses. In short, he can be, if he by no means always is, deeply rationalistic and materialistic in outlook. No one would contend that his plays set forth the precise view of the past that Thucydides expounds in the Archaeology, or the method which he contrasts to that of his predecessors in I 20–22, or the sense of historical process which he reveals in such a passage as III 82–83. Nevertheless, as the parallels show, Euripides is familiar with many of the basic ideas in all these characteristic parts of the *History*. The fact does not rob Thucydides of his originality; on the contrary, it merely confirms his truth when he said that he conceived the plan of his work at the outbreak of the war. For although he doubtless spent much of his exile pondering and developing it, yet the climate in which that plan was born was essentially the innovating, analytical, realistic climate revealed in Euripides' early plays. One must not therefore think of Thucydides as primarily an isolated figure or as one who came to his penetrating reflections merely through his own observation of a bitter war, although there is undoubtedly some justice in both these views; rather, he must appear as one who was molded in early life by the current realism of outlook towards men and states.

(2) Other and more numerous passages of Euripides show that ideas and forms of argument attributed by Thucydides to his speakers were known in Athens at or near the time when their speeches were allegedly delivered. The

parallels were taken to prove, not that the speakers used those arguments, but that they could have. Of the forms of argument, those from likelihood (εἰκός), from profit (τὸ συμφέρον), and from right (τὸ δίκαιον) were noted as especially common in Euripides and familiar to pseudo-Xenophon. And since these arguments play a prominent part in the *Rhetoric to Alexander*, they perhaps go back to Corax and Tisias and became known in Athens through Protagoras, who visited Sicily and went as a lawgiver to Thurii. It was further observed of the argument from εἰκός that, if it looks to the past in pleas of the courtroom, it must necessarily often look to the future in parliamentary speeches. Hence it forms the natural vehicle of a statesman's πρόγνωσις. Taken alone or with the argument from συμφέρον, it can likewise be used to show what men as a class tend to do, and it was seen that both of these uses, if necessarily commoner in Thucydides than in Euripides, are not unattested in the latter.

It is perhaps unnecessary to summarize in detail how Euripides confirms the ideas attributed by Thucydides to his speakers. Omitting much, one may say that there are parallels in the dramatist for Pericles' exposition of democratic theory in the Funeral Oration, for his plea for civic unity and his defense of πολυπραγμοσύνη in his third speech, for the general contrast of thought and manner in the debate between Cleon and Diodotus, for the attitude on both sides in the Melian Dialogue, and for the division between youth and age and for the difference of opinion on Syracuse in the debate between Nicias and Alcibiades. These parallels tend to show that the speeches of Thucydides are not anachronistic but that, on the contrary, they expound ideas which the historian knew to have been familiar at the time when the speeches were delivered. They therefore create a strong presumption that he thought of his speeches, not primarily as setting forth his own ideas, but as conveying the actual policies of the speakers.

Still other parallels show that Thucydides' judgment of the Spartans, of the Athenian demagogues, of Nicias, and of Alcibiades were not peculiar to himself. In these cases he has evidently tested and adopted a widespread belief.

One parallel, slender evidence as it was, appeared to suggest that Thucydides felt some impropriety in attributing to Spartans the manner of speaking which, as Euripides shows, was common at Athens. On the other hand, evidence was adduced to support the reliability, in form and content, of the Melian Dialogue.

(3) Space forbade, and forbids now, any full discussion of the rhetoric of the fifth century, but a few conclusions concerning it seemed justified. First, it was seen to be traditional; hence, it was argued, Thucydides' speeches, although his own and an organic part of his work, at the same time reflect a rhetoric generally used. Thus it need not be assumed that the speeches should have varied in style far more than they in fact do if they were to reflect speeches actually delivered by different persons. Second, it was argued that in the fifth century speakers were accustomed to look at specific circumstances in the light of the general class to which those circumstances belonged. If so, the art of rhetoric implied more than a mere skill in language; it implied an ability to understand broad laws of individual and social conduct. The point is extremely important for both authors and, I trust, can sometime be developed at greater length. But one can at least say that a broad common ground between the speeches of Thucydides and the debates of the dramatist is that in both alike the concrete issues at hand are looked on as not, so to speak, interpretable in and

through themselves, but only through the more universal laws which they exemplify.

All the arguments hitherto adduced tend to confirm what Thucydides reports was done and said in Greece during the years of which he writes. I have necessarily been concerned almost entirely with evidence favorable to his accuracy; for that is the evidence which Euripides supplies. I have notably failed to discuss the details of Thucydides' style, wherein has been found the chief argument against seeing in his speeches the true image of an earlier Athens. And it must freely be confessed that the exiled historian would have had every reason and every opportunity to achieve an abstractness peculiar to himself, and that he may besides have felt the influence of stylistic fashions which became widespread only after he left Athens. But I would urge in defense, first, that his speeches are extremely compressed. Any of them can be read in less than half an hour, whereas, to judge by extant Attic orations, speeches were commonly much longer. Thus they are to be looked on as giving the essence, not the substance, of arguments.[64] Then, second, the fullest treatment of Thucydides' language points out that the so-called Gorgian figures, although common, are not in any sense the primary instrument of his style.[65] Moreover, these figures seem to have been not unknown in Athens even before the visit there of the famous rhetorician in 427.[66] One may cite *Medea* 408–9 (cf. Soph. *Ajax* 1085–86, *O.T.* 125),

$$\gamma υ ν α \hat{ι} κ ε ς, \, \dot{ε} ς \, \mu \dot{ε} ν \, \dot{ε} σ θ λ' \, \dot{α} \mu η χ α ν ώ τ α τ α ι,$$
$$κ α κ \hat{ω} ν \, δ \dot{ε} \, π ά ν τ ω ν \, τ έ κ τ ο ν ε ς \, σ ο φ ώ τ α τ α ι,$$

[64] Cf. the judgment of Blass on the *Tetralogies* of Antiphon (*Attische Bered-samkeit*[2] I 150), "Die Reden der Tetralogien sind Skizzen wirklicher, nicht Abbilder."

[65] F. Rittelmeyer, *Thukydides und die Sophistik* (Leipzig 1915) 99–102.

[66] Navarre, 102–9 (above, n. 9), observes a great increase of these figures in Sophocles over Aeschylus, although, as Schmid remarks, the manner is merely

and the sentence attributed by Stesimbrotus to Pericles and seemingly harboring his own words (Plut. *Per.* 8 *ad fin.*), οὐ γὰρ ἐκείνους ὁρῶμεν, ἀλλὰ ταῖς τιμαῖς, ἃς ἔχουσι, καὶ τοῖς ἀγαθοῖς, ἃ παρέχουσιν, ἀθανάτους εἶναι τεκμαιρόμεθα. And finally, when we are uncertain how early the Ἀλήθεια of the sophist Antiphon is to be dated[67] or how representative the style of pseudo-Xenophon may be considered to be, it is extremely hazardous to argue on grounds of style alone that Thucydides does not in a real sense echo the Athens of Pericles. For the parallels between his *History* and the plays of Euripides make it abundantly clear both that he was himself deeply affected by ideas current there before his exile and that he attributes to his speakers thoughts and forms of argument which were equally well known.

---

an inheritance from the older Greek gnomic tradition (cf. W. Schmid and O. Stählin, *Geschichte der griechischen Literatur* [München 1934] I, 2, 483). But when the early plays of Sophocles were probably influenced by the antithetical debates of Protagoras (see above, p. 15), it is unreasonable to deny that early sophistic prose, itself inheriting the same gnomic tradition, should have been entirely a stranger to these figures. Gorgias may well have been an innovator only in the degree to which he applied what had been known before.

[67] Cf. W. Aly, "Formprobleme der frühen griechischen Prosa," *Philologus*, Supplementband 21, Heft 3 (1929) 153–54, where it is dated somewhat before the outbreak of the war. Its style is severely antithetical, far more so than that of pseudo-Xenophon. Cf. (*Vorskr.*⁹ II 347, col. 2.3–20) τὰ οὖν νόμιμα παραβαίνων εἰὰν λάθῃ τοὺς ὁμολογήσαντας, καὶ αἰσχύνης καὶ ζημίας ἀπήλλακται· μὴ λαθὼν δ' οὔ· τῶν δὲ τῇ φύσει ξυμφύτων ἐάν τι παρὰ τὸ δυνατὸν βιάζηται, ἐάν τε πάντας ἀνθρώπους λάθῃ, οὐδὲν ἔλαττον τὸ κακόν, ἐάν τε πάντες ἴδωσιν, οὐδὲν μεῖζον.

CHAPTER II

THE ORIGINS OF
THUCYDIDES' STYLE

I

In discussing the numerous resemblances of thought and
expression between Euripides and Thucydides,[1] I tried to
show that many ideas and forms of argument attributed by
Thucydides to his speakers were in fact familiar when their
speeches were allegedly delivered; for the same ideas and
arguments appear in the contemporaneous plays and fragments of Euripides. It seemed therefore to follow that
although Thucydides wrote some, perhaps most, of his
History after 404, he nevertheless reflects with some fidelity
the outlook and attitude of earlier years. One could not,
to be sure, assert on such evidence that given speakers
actually spoke as Thucydides said they did, but it was at
least clear that they might well have spoken so, since the
ideas were then so much in the air as to find expression in
tragedy. Still other resemblances between early plays of
Euripides and parts of the *History* other than the speeches
appeared to show that Thucydides was himself led to con-
ceive many of his characteristic ideas before leaving Athens,
as in the first sentence of the *History* he indeed suggests
was the case. Both conclusions seemed of some value as

[1] See above, chap. 1. Relevant passages from contemporary authors, notably
Sophocles and pseudo-Xenophon, were likewise discussed.

refuting or at least mitigating the common view that Thucydides, a more or less isolated thinker, after the end of the war put his own incisive reflections on it into the mouths of earlier statesmen. Essentially that view charges him with anachronism and derives its strength from two kinds of argument: first, that the historian at the end of the war was primarily interested in vindicating the policy of Pericles which at that time seemed to have been ruinous,[2] and then, that it was the bitter experience of war itself which bred not only in Thucydides but among Greeks generally that rhetoric and rationalism which, however, mark even the opening speeches of the *History*.[3] Now without going over the evidence again, one can at least say that the defense of democracy attributed to Pericles, the theory of oligarchy ascribed to Archidamus, the respective positions of Cleon and Diodotus (to name only what is most striking) find close parallels in the plays of Euripides before and during the Archidamian War; and what is more important, that the considerations of power, the arguments from τὸ συμφέρον, the use of εἰκός to show what is generically true of men or states—in short, the characteristic means by which Thucydides and his speakers reveal their rationalistic outlook—are not less attested in the same period. There seems therefore a very real error in underrating the rationalism and the skill in argument which, as is clear from the *Medea* of 431, already marked the Athens of Pericles. If so, then even the speeches of the first books may well be thought to reflect, not primarily the author's later views or a rhetoric which developed later, but rather the ways of the contemporary mind.

But even if the view thus inadequately sketched were accepted, the objection would soon arise that in style at

[2] Ed. Schwartz, *Das Geschichtswerk des Thukydides*[2] (Bonn 1929) 133.
[3] Wilamowitz, *Aristoteles und Athen* (Berlin 1893) I 176.

least the speeches of the first books cannot be faithful to the period which they purport to represent. The antithetical sentences of Pericles, for instance, have usually been described as Gorgian, but Pericles died in 429, two years before the famous embassy on which Gorgias first dazzled the Athenians. Blass accordingly was led to state,[4] "Die Leichenrede bei Thukydides und die beiden andern daselbst dem Perikles in den Mund gelegten Reden geben uns von dem Geiste des Mannes ein treues Abbild, von seiner Beredsamkeit nicht," and Alfred Croiset,[5] Steup,[6] and two scholars who have most fully discussed Thucydides' style, Rittelmeyer[7] and Ros,[8] echo his words directly or, by calling the style Gorgian, indirectly. Hence the issue seems quite clear: either Gorgias introduced antithetical prose into Athens in 427, in which case the style of speeches representing a period before and doubtless immediately after that date is in fact anachronistic, or Pericles spoke in some such way as Thucydides said he spoke, in which case the innovations of Gorgias, however significant in some respects, were nevertheless not so far-reaching as has been supposed.

But thus baldly put, the alternative seems somewhat unreal. Could one man, it may be asked, make such a change so quickly? Can one year stand as a dividing line between literary styles, which by their nature are merely instruments to express pervading and therefore slow changes in men's outlook? For however brilliant or startling the innovations of an individual may be, they owe their acceptance (the more so if it be rapid) to some state of readiness or

---

[4] *Die attische Beredsamkeit*[2] (Leipzig 1887) I 34.
[5] *Thucydide, Livres I–II* (Paris 1886) 104–6, 110, 114–15.
[6] Classen-Steup, *Thukydides*[5] (1919) I, lxxx, though his statements are more guarded than the foregoing.
[7] *Thukydides und die Sophistik* (Leipzig 1915), esp. 36–51, 93–102.
[8] *Die μεταβολή als Stilprinzip des Thukydides* (Paderborn 1938) p. 1. But see below, pp. 112–17.

preparation in the public mind. So considered, the question rather becomes: were there no antecedents of the Gorgian style; for if not, then the changes wrought by Gorgias were almost unprecedented in their speed and thoroughness. Consider, for example, a fragment of the orator Antiphon almost certainly from a speech of the year 425:[9] καίτοι οὐκ ἂν τῆς μὲν τῶν ἄλλων πολιτῶν ταλαιπωρίας προύσκέψαντο, τῆς δὲ σφετέρας αὐτῶν ἑταιρίας οὐκ ἐνεθυμήθησαν. Must one say that so pointed an antithesis would have been foreign to the prose of two years past, and that, although it was composed by an experienced advocate then probably in his fifties for persuasion, not for show? Undoubtedly it would be easier to believe that Antiphon did not in 427 suddenly adopt an unfamiliar and, if so, probably a repellent style, but rather that certain of the so-called Gorgianisms were already known before the rhetorician came to Athens. If it could be shown that they were, then Gorgias would appear less as the bringer of something wholly new than as a man of brilliant virtuosity who systematized, heightened, and carried farther usages known before but never so boldly sought. Yet exactly that fact would, if admitted, have the greatest bearing on the origin of Thucydides' style. For one would no longer be compelled to think of his antitheses as Gorgian and, therefore, as anachronistic in the speeches of the early books. On the contrary, his style, like the arguments of his speeches and many of his own ideas, would in its essentials appear to reflect the Athens which he knew in the thirties and twenties before his exile.

II

Perhaps the easiest and clearest means of discussing the question will be first to examine the more important

[9] L. Gernet, *Antiphon* (Paris 1923) fg. 4, p. 165; cf. also p. 161 on the date of the Περὶ τοῦ Σαμοθρᾳκων φόρου.

opinions advanced in ancient and modern times on the innovations of Gorgias, and at the same time to appraise those opinions by comparing them with one another and with such other evidence as seems relevant. Then another section will be devoted to the fragments of the sophist Antiphon which, if, as seems probable, they antedate the arrival of Gorgias in Athens, should serve both to test the conclusions achieved thus far and to present a concrete, if limited, example of the sophistic prose composed in Athens during Thucydides' early manhood. Finally, in a brief conclusion the evidence on the question, how far the style of Thucydides' speeches is representative of the period in which they were allegedly delivered, will be collected and summarized.

The most categorical statement made in ancient times on the innovations of Gorgias and the one which undoubtedly has been most influential is that of Diodorus. His source is usually taken to be Timaeus, mentioned by Dionysius in his somewhat similar account. But since Dionysius expressly hesitates to speak so categorically, the sweeping statement of Diodorus is not beyond suspicion. Moreover, one must remember that it appears in a compendium of history. Had Diodorus known the several steps in the development of Attic style, he doubtless would not have reported them in such a work, and as it was, Gorgias was sufficiently celebrated to appear in a general way as the εὑρετής of artistic prose. The statement of Diodorus follows (XII 53): Gorgias, he says, was the most eminent rhetorician of his day; on his arrival in Athens with the deputation from Leontini, τῷ ξενίζοντι τῆς λέξεως ἐξέπληξε τοὺς Ἀθηναίους ὄντας εὐφυεῖς καὶ φιλολόγους. πρῶτος γὰρ ἐχρήσατο τοῖς τῆς λέξεως σχηματισμοῖς περιττοτέροις καὶ τῇ φιλοτεχνίᾳ διαφέρουσιν, ἀντιθέτοις καὶ ἰσοκώλοις καὶ παρίσοις καὶ ὁμοιοτελεύτοις καί τισιν ἑτέροις τοιούτοις, ἃ τότε μὲν διὰ τὸ ξένον τῆς κατασκευῆς ἀποδοχῆς ἠξιοῦντο, νῦν δὲ περιεργίαν ἔχειν δοκεῖ κτλ. In short, Gorgias was the first to use the so-called Gorgian figures, which were unknown in Athens before he introduced them but promptly accepted thereafter. Dionysius was less certain. He says (*Lys.* 3): ἥψατο δὲ καὶ τῶν Ἀθήνησι ῥητόρων ἡ ποιητική τε καὶ τροπικὴ φράσις, ὡς μὲν Τίμαιός φησι, Γοργίου ἄρξαντος ἡνίκ' Ἀθήναζε πρεσβεύων κατέπληξε τοὺς ἀκούοντας τῇ δημηγορίᾳ, ὡς δὲ τἀληθὲς ἔχει, τὸ καὶ παλαιότερον αἰεί τι θαυμαζομένη.[10] Evidently he could not feel sure how far Gorgias introduced a new style of speaking, because he did not question the essential accuracy of the speeches ascribed by the historian to Pericles, yet observed in them certain Gorgian traits. He in fact well expresses the dilemma regarding the speeches of Thucydides which was set forth above.

Cicero, with what significance it is hard to tell, names Thrasymachus before Gorgias as having systematically employed antithesis, parison, and the like (*Orat.* 12.39; cf. 13.40), though he undoubtedly thought the latter's style more marked by these figures (52.175). Now Thrasymachus is mentioned in a fragment of the Δαιταλῆς[11] produced early in 427 some months before the deputation from Leontini reached Athens in the autumn of the same year (Thuc. III 86). Since Aristophanes would hardly have chosen the new rhetoric as the subject of his first play unless it had been well known, Cicero's statement thus gains a certain strength. Yet he doubtless made no such close

---

[10] But he names only Polus and Licymnius as practicing such a style (*Thuc.* 24, *Ep. II ad Amm.* 2) and elsewhere links the names of Thucydides and Gorgias (*Demosth.* 4 and 6; *Ep. ad Pomp.* 2.8).

[11] Fg. 168, Kock.

calculations of date. No more should probably be deduced from his words than that he or someone from whom he gained his information[12] knew that Thrasymachus, who certainly was in Athens before Gorgias, used the Gorgian figures, though in moderation. Thus, if in itself Cicero's statement gives little that is certain, it at least undermines the seeming certainty of Diodorus. That Gorgias in one visit and by a few orations suddenly changed the whole course of Attic prose seems the less probable the more one considers the plot of the Δαιταλῆς and the later fame of Thrasymachus.

As one turns from these later citations to those of a period nearer the events in question, much less is heard of Gorgias' innovations. There can be little doubt that no early tradition existed in Athens concerning the importance of the visit of 427. Gorgias is often mentioned, not unnaturally since he lived into the fourth century, visited Athens several times, left such disciples there as Isocrates and Alcidamas, and in his declining years became doubtless to many, as he did to Plato, the great symbol of rhetorical education. Aristotle (*Rhet.* III 1.1404a24) cites his poetical style to illustrate an early stage in the development of artistic prose; apparently he considered it not necessarily the only or the first, but rather the best example of the tendency which he is describing. But he was less concerned with style than with argument, and it is perhaps significant that he attributes the development of κοινοὶ τόποι equally to Protagoras and to Gorgias (*Rhet.* II 24.1402a23; cf. *Soph. El.* 34.183b37; Plato, *Phaedrus* 216b, 267a). Yet Protagoras was in Athens probably as early as 450, and since the technical part of his teaching

---

[12] He elsewhere mentions Aristotle and Theophrastus (*Orat.* 51.172, 57.194), the latter of whom is known to have discussed the style of Thrasymachus (Dion. *Lys.* 6).

evidently resembled that of Gorgias, it is hard to believe that his style, on the other hand, was quite different.[13]

Plato, rather than describe Gorgias' style, consciously imitates it in the *Symposium* in the speech of Agathon.[14] From the point of view of chronology, the speech is especially interesting since it shows that a person who reached maturity after the Peace of Nicias was most influenced by Gorgias, a fact abundantly confirmed by the fragments of Agathon[15] and possibly by the similarities between the Ἑλένης Ἐγκώμιον and the speech of Helen in the *Trojan Women*, produced in 415.[16] Thus, if one is to speak of a thoroughgoing influence of Gorgias in Athens—an influence which inspired pleasure not so much in logical antithesis as in the mannerisms of short balanced clauses, rhyme, and wordplay—then one finds it first in Agathon. But Plato certainly did not think that antithesis as such was Gorgian. On the contrary, in the *Protagoras*, the dramatic date of which is before the outbreak of the war, he attributes highly antithetical sentences to Prodicus (*Protag.* 337a–c2), as does Xenophon in the *Memorabilia* (II 1.21–34). Thus if, as is usually believed, Plato tried to be true to history in the setting of his dialogues, we must take it that he distinguished an earlier use of antithesis, which he thought typical of the older sophists, from the mannered and rhymed antitheses of Gorgias, which he considered characteristic of the generation of Agathon.

Moreover, certain facts known to ourselves seem to confirm Plato's judgment. First, although, as will be shown

---

[13] See below, pp. 70, 73–84, 105–8.
[14] 194e4–197e8. Cf. 198c, καὶ γάρ με Γοργίου ὁ λόγος ἀνεμίμνῃσκεν, and the following pun on the Γοργίου κεφαλή.
[15] Esp. fgs. 6, 9, 11, 12, 27, 29 (Nauck² 1926).
[16] Possibly also by the fact that in the *Birds* of 414 Aristophanes first speaks of Gorgias at some length (1694–1705). He mentions him briefly in the *Wasps*, line 421.

below,[17] the early extant plays of both Sophocles and Euripides reveal abundant and conscious antithesis, these poets never assumed the mannerisms of Agathon. In other words, they acquired their styles in a period when antithesis was common and did not succumb to the extreme and truly Gorgian symmetry of a later generation. Then, the antithetical style of the orator Antiphon may well have been fully formed by 427. At least, Aly's attempt[18] to date the *Tetralogies* after 428 on the ground that the εἰσφοραί mentioned in *Tetralogy* A, β, 12, necessarily follow the εἰσφορά which Thucydides says was first voted in that year (III 19.1) cannot be accepted. For an orderly procedure governing such levies is already recognized in the second part of the well-known decree of Callias (*IG* I² 92, lines 48, 50), now generally dated in 434/3.[19] Thus Thucydides means that the εἰσφορά of 428 was the first to be raised in the course of the war, not in the course of Attic history,[20] and the imaginary defendant of the first *Tetralogy* speaks of an institution quite accepted in the Periclean Age. But the absence of a *terminus post quem* does not, of course, in itself place the *Tetralogies* before 427, and although it is impossible to consider here in any detail the vexed question of their date, it can at least be said that, because of their more poetical language and greater number of Ionisms, the *Tetralogies* have been commonly accepted as the earliest of the orator's

[17] Pages 75–85.
[18] "Formprobleme der frühen griechischen Prosa," *Philologus*, Supplementband 21, Heft 3 (1929) 116.
[19] W. Kolbe, "Das Kalliasdekret," *Sitzungsber. d. Berl. Akad.* (1927) 319ff = *Thukydides im Lichte der Urkunden* (Stuttgart 1930) 50–67. Kolbe's dating is accepted by W. S. Ferguson, *The Treasurers of Athena* (Cambridge, Mass. 1932) 153, and B. D. Meritt, *AJP* 55 (1934) 263, who reports (*ibid.*, p. 272) the agreement also of H. T.Wade-Gery in spite of the latter's previous argument (*JHS* 51 [1931] 57–85) for the year 422/1.
[20] So *RE* X 2150 s.v. εἰσφορά. This interpretation of Thucydides is quite natural since he previously (I 141.5, II 13.3–6) emphasizes the huge surplus with which Athens entered the war.

Three Essays on Thucydides

extant works.[21] Certainly, the fact that Protagoras and Pericles are reported (Plut. *Per.* 36) to have discussed the same subject as is treated in the second *Tetralogy* tells something of the period when such subjects were of interest,[22] and the pervasive religiosity of all three works, as well as their extreme reliance on the oldest of the sophistic arguments, that of εἰκός, again point to an early date. Then, the contrast of tone between the impassioned third speech of the second *Tetralogy* and the carefully reasoned fourth speech[23] offers a close parallel not only, as will appear below, to the debate between Cleon and Diodotus in Thucydides but also to two debates of tragedy, namely, those between Oedipus and Creon in the *Oedipus Rex* (513–615) and between Theseus and Hippolytus (*Hipp.* 936–1035). In all four cases one sees violent accusation answered by clear and close argument,[24] and since the reasoning which these debates of tragedy reflect is undoubtedly sophistic (both Creon and Hippolytus use the argument from εἰκός),[25] it seems natural to think of the *Tetralogies* as preceding either of the plays. For theorists must have been elaborating their new methods of proof for some time before these became sufficiently well known to find a place in tragedy. Further arguments for the *Tetralogies'* early date may be found in their undoubted difference in language from the orator's later speeches—a difference which has led certain scholars to deny the

---

[21] Cf. J. H. Thiel, *Antiphons erste Tetralogie* (Den Haag 1932) 13.
[22] The subject seems to have come up also in Euripides' *Telephus* of 438. Cf. Hyginus *Fab.* 101 (quoted by Nauck² p. 579), where it is stated that the Achaean chiefs begged Achilles to heal Telephus; *quibus Achilles respondit se artem medicam non nosse. tunc Ulixes ait: non te dicit Apollo, sed auctorem vulneris hastam nominat. quam cum rasissent, remediatus est.*
[23] In *Tetr.* B, δ, 2 the speaker refers to his arguments as λεπτὰ . . . καὶ ἀκριβῆ. Jason uses the same words in his debate with Medea (*Med.* 529, 532).
[24] Cf. above, chap. 1 pp. 31–32.
[25] See below, n. 28.

Tetralogies to Antiphon,[26] but which seems quite explicable on the assumption of a lapse of time between the two classes of works[27]—and also in the fact that Thucydides, exiled in 424, knew and admired Antiphon (VIII 68.1–2), who thus was presumably active as a writer during the historian's earlier life in Athens. These indications are doubtless not conclusive, and a new and thorough attempt to date the *Tetralogies* is much to be desired.[28] Nevertheless, they do tend to confirm Drerup's suggestion that the *Tetralogies* were composed about 430 and thus to reinforce his view, of which more will be said later,[29] that their style is quite free from the special Gorgian traits.

[26] So Gernet (above, n. 9) pp. 6–16, where references are given to earlier writings.

[27] So Thiel (above, n. 21) 5–19.

[28] Interesting recent attempts are those of Thiel (pp. 19–22; see above, n. 21), who argues for a date shortly after 427, and of F. Schupp ("Zur Geschichte der Beweistopik in der älteren griechischen Gerichtsrede," *Wiener Studien* 45 [1926] 17–28, 173–85), who thinks that the *Palamedes* of Gorgias precedes the *Tetralogies* and thus would place them nearer 420 (pp. 177–80). But Thiel's arguments are largely stylistic, and if this paper has any merit, the mere presence of antithesis in the *Tetralogies* does not suffice to place them after the visit of Gorgias. On the other hand, Schupp's valuable paper, in which he treats the proofs used by Gorgias, Antiphon, and others, is impaired by his failure to consider the early plays and fragments of Euripides. Thus he argues that Gorgias broadened the topic of εἰκός to include four aspects of any crime—namely, the person, act, place, and time (πρόσωπον, πρᾶγμα, τόπος, χρόνος)—and suggests that this method became known in Athens only after 427. But in the *Hippolytus* of 428, the hero covers the first two of these subjects in answering the charges of his father, arguing, in lines 993–1006, that a person of his σωφροσύνη would not have been likely to commit such a crime and, in lines 1007–20, that the crime itself would have brought him no advantage. The theory of εἰκός and the use of τεκμήρια are set forth again in fgs. 811 and 812 of the *Phoenix*, which, being mentioned in the *Acharnians* (line 421), was produced at the latest at the Great Dionysia of 426 only a half year after Gorgias' arrival and, quite as probably, somewhat earlier. The second of these fragments contains further resemblances to Antiphon in the suggestion that a man is normally true to his φύσις (cf. *Tetr.* B, γ, 1) and that εἰκότα are quite as important as the testimony of witnesses (*Tetr.* A, α, 9). Examples of Schupp's three other topics, σύγκρισις (i.e. the argument *a maiore, a minore*, or from the opposite), ὁρισμός (definition), δίλημμα (alternatives) are likewise found in the early plays of Euripides. For the first, cf. *Med.* 490–91, 586–87, *Philoctetes* fg. 794; for the second, *Bellerophon* fg. 297; for the third, *ibid.* fg. 292, *Ino* fg. 407. Since, as has been remarked, the use of such arguments in tragedy implies that they were already somewhat familiar to the general public, a theorist such as Antiphon should probably be imagined as writing earlier rather than later.

[29] Pages 70–72.

Again, in a well-known passage of the Mytilenean Debate (III 38.3; summer 427) Thucydides makes Cleon accuse the Athenians of an empty love of rhetoric. Like Aristophanes in the Δαιταλῆς of the same year, he therefore testifies to the prominence of rhetoric before the arrival of Gorgias, and though in an essay on the historicity of Thucydides' style, it would obviously be reasoning in a circle to adduce the balanced clauses of Diodotus as typical of the rhetoric to which Cleon alludes, nevertheless it is in fact difficult to think of that rhetoric in any other context than that of Antiphon's *Tetralogies*, Cicero's testimony concerning Thrasymachus, and Plato's parody of Prodicus, the more so since the peculiarly antithetical style of Diodotus confirms the rest of the evidence. In short, the Mytilenean Debate offers a test case of the stylistic veracity of Thucydides' speeches; for when Cleon attacks rhetoric and Diodotus replies in cool antithetical sentences quite evidently intended to illustrate a rhetorical training, then to doubt the style means virtually to doubt the substance of the debate. Finally, contrasting the present generation with the older breed of the Μαραθωνομάχαι personified by the chorus, Aristophanes in the *Acharnians* (686) represents the former as speaking στρογγύλοις τοῖς ῥήμασιν. The best commentary on the word στρογγύλος, "well-rounded," "periodic," appears in the *Phaedrus* (234e), where Socrates uses it to describe the foregoing speech which the young Phaedrus had taken from Lysias, a speech which by its formal use of τεκμήρια and εἰκότα and by its rigid antithetical style is apparently designed to portray or mimic the rhetorical methods pursued by Lysias before he turned λογογράφος. In any case, this word well shows what Aristophanes in 425 considered the current oratorical style, and though the citation postdates the first visit of Gorgias by something over a year, still, as in the case of Antiphon's *Tetralogies*, it is hard to credit to one man and one visit a phenonemon apparently so general. Thus, when Plato distinguishes between an earlier antithetical style of sophists present in Athens before the war and the later more precious symmetry of Gorgias which he ascribes to Agathon in the period after the Peace of Nicias, other evidence from the years in question seems to confirm his judgment.

We may now pass from the ancient testimony on the influence of Gorgias in Athens to more recent opinions on the subject. Blass, as was remarked,[30] laying great weight on the statement of Diodorus, attributed antithetical prose as such to the influence of Gorgias, which he accordingly found in the *Tetralogies* of Antiphon and the speeches of Thucydides. Quite consistently he thought the actual speeches of Pericles could not have resembled those ascribed to him by the historian. And scholars concerned more narrowly with Thucydides accepted Blass's position by calling the historian's style Gorgian because it is antithetical. But other students of rhetoric, notably Norden, Navarre, Drerup, and Aly, advanced a different view.

Impressed by the antithetical nature of Greek speech as such but more particularly by the antitheses, which he listed, in the early plays of Euripides, Norden[31] sought and, as he believed, found the prototypes of the Gorgian figures in Heraclitus, arguing that other sophists as well as Gorgias underwent the latter's influence. Thus, he concluded his remarks on the early sophists by saying,[32] "Das gemeinsame Band, welches sie alle umschliesst, ist der Kampf gegen das traditionell Bestehende, und er findet seinen sinnlichen Ausdruck in der antithetischen Sprache." Again, alluding to

[30] Above, p. 57.
[31] *Die antike Kunstprosa* (Leipzig 1898) I 17-41.
[32] *Ibid.*, p. 20.

the language of the *Medea* of 431, he said:[33] "Nur das können wir mit Sicherheit schliessen, dass durch den Einfluss der in Athen sich aufhaltenden Sophisten die attische Rede schon vor Gorgias durch künstliche Mittel gehoben war." But he contented himself with these pregnant remarks, not attempting to pursue their full implications.

Navarre,[34] two years after Norden but apparently in ignorance of his work, treated the rhetorical and sophistic movements of the Periclean Age in greater detail, but although he thus amassed more evidence concerning the style of the period, he failed to interpret it with Norden's insight. Nevertheless, he established at the start one point of great importance, namely, that no rigid line could be drawn, as it had been by Blass and Jebb, between the Ionian dialectic of the earlier sophists and the Sicilian rhetoric of the later.[35] For, as he showed, the ties between Athens and the West were close after the founding of Thurii where Protagoras lived as lawgiver and Tisias is said to have taught. Moreover, Protagoras himself visited Sicily,[36] evolved κοινοὶ τόποι similar to those of Gorgias and, as has been said, is reported to have discussed with Pericles the same case of the boy killed accidentally by a javelin that Antiphon treats in his second *Tetralogy*.[37] Moreover, the early plays of Euripides confirm the existence of the Sicilian arguments in Athens before the arrival of Gorgias.[38] Thus Navarre[39] could speak of a whole generation between 450 and 430, "qui dans sa façon de raisonner, comme aussi dans les procédés de son langage, a été marquée pas les sophistes d'une empreinte ineffaçable.

---

[33] *Ibid.*, p. 29.
[34] *Essai sur la Rhétorique Grecque avant Aristote*, Paris 1900.
[35] *Ibid.*, pp. 21–23.
[36] [Plato] *Hipp. Mai.* 282d.
[37] Plut. *Per.* 36. Stesimbrotus, mentioned just below, appears to be Plutarch's authority.
[38] See above, n. 28.   [39] Pages 24–25.

Cette action des Protagoras, des Prodicos, des Hippias, elle éclate dans l'histoire d'un Thucydide comme dans la poésie d'un Euripide; si nous avions conservé quelques unes des oeuvres oratoires de ce temps-là, par exemple celles de Périclès, nul doute qu'elle ne s'y montrât au même degré."

But Navarre was less convincing when he went on to discuss the style of the early sophists, the chief traits of which he listed as poetic diction, amplitude, and distinction in the meaning of words.[40] Yet a few pages later he declared that the antecedents of the Gorgian style are to be found in tragedy, notably in the early plays of Sophocles, which he contrasted with those of Aeschylus by saying,[41] "Une première différence, c'est que le nombre de ces figures, ou du moins de certaines d'entre elles, y est infiniment plus considérable," and again,[42] "l'antithèse, rare chez Eschyle, est un des procédés favoris de Sophocle." And through several pages he carefully listed the examples of antithesis and paronomasia in the *Antigone*. Thus he adduced, though with greater thoroughness, essentially the same evidence as Norden, yet failed to draw Norden's conclusion that this great advance in reasoned antithetical speech in Sophocles and Euripides over Aeschylus was inspired by the sophistic movement and therefore must reflect its style. On the contrary, he merely concluded that Sophocles was Gorgias' model, not inquiring why Sophocles himself abandoned the magniloquent, poetic tradition of the past for the more exacting, more intellectual manner of the *Antigone*. But even on his own view of the style fostered by the earlier sophists, it is hard to see how the practice of distinguishing between synonyms did not conduce to an antithetical style.

[40] Pages 67–68.
[41] Page 102.   [42] Page 106.

Certainly Plato in his parody of Prodicus suggests that it did, as does Xenophon,[43] and the examples of Prodican distinctions in Euripides[44] and Thucydides[45] fall naturally into antithesis. For, after all, antithesis is nothing more than an effective means of isolating and therefore clarifying concepts, and its vogue in fifth-century style, if it grew to be artificial seemingly through Gorgias' influence, at bottom springs from the desire for forceful clarity.[46] Thus, not only the distinctions of Prodicus but the ὀρθοέπεια and ἀντιλογίαι[47] of Protagoras, being likewise attempts to clarify the substance and expression of ideas (in the latter case, of contrasting ideas), seem hardly imaginable except as one posits a widespread use of such style as that of the famous sentence, πάντων χρημάτων μέτρον ἐστὶν ἄνθρωπος, τῶν μὲν ὄντων ὡς ἔστιν, τῶν δὲ οὐκ ὄντων ὡς οὐκ ἔστιν.[48] Hence, in regard to the style fostered by the early generation of sophists, Navarre, despite his usual penetration, seems himself to present the evidence by which his own view can be questioned.

Norden and Navarre, then, pointed to tragedy as a source of information on prose style, a legitimate and fruitful procedure since the tragedians were in close touch with all the great contemporary movements, rhetoric not least. Their successor Drerup,[49] on the other hand, largely confined himself to the notices concerning the early rhetoricians and to their actual fragments, when in a brilliant essay he sought to show that the rudiments of two styles existed in

[43] See above, p. 62.
[44] Cf. H. Mayer, *Prodikos von Keos* (Paderborn 1913) 48–54.
[45] Cf. I 69.6; II 62.4; III 39.2, 72.1, 82.4.
[46] Cf. Arist. *Rhet.* III 9.8: ἡδεῖα δ' ἐστὶν ἡ τοιαύτη λέξις, ὅτι τἀναντία γνωριμώτατα καὶ παράλληλα μᾶλλον γνώριμα.
[47] *Vorsokr.*9 II, fg. 5 (p. 265).
[48] *Ibid.*, fg. 1 (p. 263).
[49] "Theodoros von Byzanz," *Jahrbücher f. class. Philologie*, Supplementband 27 (1902) 219–372.

the late Periclean Age: the one, the truly periodic style of Thrasymachus which, though it used antithesis, included it in a rhythmical and rounded whole, and the other and earlier, the antithetical style as such, which aimed at no larger periodic framework. This latter style he regarded as the offspring of eristic[50]—"Sie beruht auf der gegensätzlichen Entwicklung der Gedanken in der Antithese, die in der sophistischen Prosa zu einer Grundlage stilistischer Kunst geprägt worden ist, nachdem sie längst schon von den Vorläufern der Sophisten, einem Heraklit und Zenon, gekannt war." And he argued that it was wholly from this sophistic inheritance, not from Gorgias, that Antiphon derived the antithetical style of his *Tetralogies*; for the originality of Gorgias was not to have created that style but to have embellished it. Accordingly he recognized the latter's influence only in the artificial heightening of the antithesis by means of rhyme and wordplay, concluding,[51] "Deshalb ist es eine sonderbare Verkennung der Grund-bedingungen dieses Stiles, wenn man allgemein mit der antiken Stilkritik die Antithese zu den eigentlichen gorgian-ischen 'Figuren' rechnet. Gorgias hat vielmehr den Gegensatz zur Grundlage seines Stiles genommen und auf dieser Grundlage das complizierte System der schmücken-den Figuren aufgebaut, indem er die in der Antithese sich entwickelnden Wortkünsteleien und Klangwirkungen mit Anlehnung an die Kunstmittel der Dichtersprache syste-matisch ausbildete." This statement stands as a kind of landmark; for it expounds with force and clarity the view adumbrated by Norden but for the most part still neglected, that the antithesis is not in itself Gorgian but a stylistic principle which Gorgias merely developed. Moreover,

[50] *Ibid.*, p. 224.
[51] *Ibid.*, p. 261; cf. p. 289.

Drerup regarded that principle as to some extent dictating its own effects; for in noting the πάρισα and παρόμοια of the *Tetralogies*, he could say that they arose not through the conscious application of Gorgian rules (the developed Gorgian figures of the *Helen* and the *Palamedes* being on the whole absent) but were rather[52] "das Produkt einer natürlichen rednerischen Veranlagung und einer scharfen logischeristischen Schulung des Verstandes." In other words, granted what was remarked in the last paragraph, that antithesis and parallelism are the readiest instruments of clarity, then a mind trained in eristic debate and grappling with the logic of Sicilian argument would of itself tend to symmetry of expression, the more so since Greek not only supplied the connectives τε-τε, μὲν-δέ but the natural assonances of the verbal and nominal endings. But if one accepts the argument so far, then its application to the style of Thucydides is obvious. Though he expressly abstained from discussing it in detail, Drerup remarks that it[53] "auf denselben Elementen beruht, wie die ältere sophistische Kunstprosa [i.e. pre-Gorgian prose] und aus ihr ganz offenbar abgeleitet ist." In other words, one should not, like Rittelmeyer[54] or indeed Dionysius, consider the historian's antitheses, parallelisms, and occasional assonances as in themselves Gorgian, since they appear likewise in the *Tetralogies*. Rather on such a theory these figures would reflect the sophistic influences current in Thucydides' youth and apparent in tragedy before 427, whereas the later influence of Gorgias could be shown only insofar as the special Gorgian traits—short equal clauses, abundant word-play, consistent rhyme—likewise appear.

[52] *Ibid.*, p. 288.
[53] *Ibid.*, p. 332.
[54] See above, p. 57.

Finally, it will be necessary to speak at greater length of Aly's[55] very suggestive monograph, though it seems more valuable for the study of Antiphon than of pre-Gorgian prose, on which it is neither easy to follow nor seemingly quite consistent. On the one hand, Aly speaks of Protagoras, in Athens shortly after 450, as "der Schöpfer der perikleischen Geistigkeit" (p. 133); attributes to him the concept of the unwritten laws (pp. 133, 173) and the contemporary theory of democracy (p. 103); finds in his use of the dialogue and of the antilogy Thucydides' model respectively for the Melian Dialogue and the pairing of speeches (pp. 95–101) and in general considers his influence that which "die Denkform des Thukydides von der des Herodot scheidet" (p. 102). Further, he stresses the rise of oratory after the middle of the century (p. 179) and admits the use of certain Gorgian figures in that period (p. 75), since they appear in the Περὶ Ὁμονοίας of the sophist Antiphon which he follows Altwegg in dating as early as 439 (p. 153).[56] On the other hand, he thinks of Protagoras as having a figurative and poetic style and as often expounding his ideas by myths (though it is not clear how such a style or method comports with the logical content of his thought, which accordingly Aly, despite the examples of Heraclitus and Parmenides, declares incapable of real abstraction, p. 173). Similarly, he emphasizes the imagery and the poeticisms of Pericles (p. 81), dismissing any possible stylistic resemblances to the speeches given by Thucydides (p. 79); finally, he says that Gorgias introduced the argument from εἰκός (pp. 53, 176) and that rhetorical theory reached Athens in the twenties (*ibid.*).

Now undoubtedly Aly has a very real feeling, nurtured by his studies of Herodotus, for archaic and popular

---

[55] For reference, see above, n. 18.
[56] See below, pp. 92–96.

expression; yet he seems too much influenced by Herodotus and too little by tragedy. As has been remarked,[57] the *Hippolytus* of 428 and the *Oedipus Rex*, commonly dated at about the same time,[58] use the argument from ἐικός, as does the *Phoenix* (fgs. 811, 812), produced at the latest in 426 and very possibly somewhat earlier.[59] Indeed, as Drerup remarked,[60] the argument was probably used from the first by Protagoras, being the most natural means of strengthening the ἥττων λόγος. The use of τεκμήρια, another Sicilian device, is probably attested in the 'Αλήθεια,[61] dated by Aly himself in the thirties,[62] and certainly in the fragments of the *Phoenix* cited above. Pericles himself uses the device in the famous sentence on the dead in the Samian War, the exact wording of which seems to have been quoted by Plutarch from Stesimbrotus (*Per.* 8 *ad fin.*), οὐ γὰρ ἐκείνους ὁρῶμεν, ἀλλὰ ταῖς τιμαῖς, ἃς ἔχουσι, καὶ τοῖς ἀγαθοῖς, ἃ παρέχουσιν, ἀθανάτους εἶναι τεκμαιρόμεθα. In passing, the antithetical arrangement and the assonance of ἔχουσι and παρέχουσιν should be noticed in this sentence. Thus Aly is incorrect in ascribing the Sicilian arguments to Gorgias.

Then again, if one turn to the debate of the *Medea* of 431, an ἅμιλλα λόγων (546) between the heroine and Jason in which the latter, as the chorus remarks (576), expounds the ἥττων λόγος, it is at once apparent that Aly underrates the

[57] Above, pp. 64–65.
[58] Cf. Schmid-Stählin, *Gesch. d. griech. Lit.*, I, 2 (1934), p. 361; M. Pohlenz, *Griech. Trag.*, II 63; T. B. L. Webster, *Sophocles*, pp. 4–5. Webster well observes the close similarity of the debates in the two plays cited above, p. 64. Since the arguments of Hippolytus transcend and include those of Creon, the *Hippolytus* would appear to be the later play (so D. Grene, "The Interpretation of the *Hippolytus* of Euripides," *CP* 34 [1939] 53).
[59] See above, n. 28.
[60] "Theodoros von Byzanz," pp. 221–22.
[61] *Vorsokr.*9 II, fg. 44, col. 5.1–17 (pp. 349–50), where examples are given to confirm a general statement.
[62] See below, pp. 97–103.

conscious rhetoric of the Periclean Age. Medea, like Cleon in the Mytilenean Debate (III 39) or the Corinthians at Athens (esp. I 40–41), relies on the argument from τὸ δίκαιον. After stating her husband's shamelessness, she proves it, as do the aforementioned speakers, by retailing her past benefits to him (465–95); she then goes on to an appeal to the emotions of the sort attributed to Thrasymachus, and concludes by exclaiming on the wickedness of men (496–519). Jason (522–75), like Diodotus (III 46–47) and the Corcyreans (I 33), relies on the arguments from τὸ συμφέρον and from the irresistibility of natural impulses.[63] Being the second speaker, he adopts a technique of rebuttal similar to that of Antiphon (*Tetr.* A, β, 1–9)[64] and, after a brief introduction, refutes her arguments in detail (522–44); then, again like the Corcyreans (I 32.1), he states what he must prove[65] and does so, concluding with an attack on women (569–75) which balances Medea's opposite conclusion.[66] Here then is a perfect example of the pairing of speeches which Aly attributes to Protagoras and considers Thucydides' model, and in fact, as has been said, the speeches have many Thucydidean traits. But quite evidently the rhetorical structure followed by Euripides is more developed than Aly asserts; hence by his own argument the rhetoric taught in Athens by Protagoras was by no means simple, and one can no more say that Gorgias was the first to introduce rhetorical principles than one can attribute the Sicilian arguments to him.

---

[63] For a fuller discussion see above, chap. 1 pp. 11–13, 29–33.

[64] Cf. also the opening paragraphs of the Corinthians (I 37–39) and of Diodotus (III 42–43).

[65] Lines 548–50, ἐν τῷδε δείξω πρῶτα μὲν σοφὸς γεγώς, | ἔπειτα σώφρων, εἶτα σοὶ μέγας φίλος | καὶ παισὶ τοῖς ἐμοῖσιν.

[66] I omit discussion of the similar debate in the *Hippolytus* in which Phaedra relies on the argument from τὸ καλόν (373–430), and the nurse, very much like Diodotus (III 45), rejoins by stating the irresistibility of natural impulses (433–81). See below, pp. 99–100, and above, chap. 1 pp. 29–33.

But the structure of the debate in the *Medea* leads on to its style; for just as Medea's and Jason's speeches outwardly balance each other, so internally they often fall into balanced and symmetrical clauses. Such sentences as those of Jason (569–73),

> ἀλλ' ἐς τοσοῦτον ἥκεθ' ὥστ' ὀρθουμένης
> εὐνῆς γυναῖκες πάντ' ἔχειν νομίζετε,
> ἢν δ' αὖ γένηται ξυμφορά τις ἐς λέχος,
> τὰ λῷστα καὶ κάλλιστα πολεμιώτατα
> τίθεσθε,

and (601–2),

> τὰ χρηστὰ μή σοι λυπρὰ φαίνεσθαί ποτε,
> μηδ' εὐτυχοῦσα δυστυχὴς εἶναι δοκεῖν,

only exemplify a common practice confirmed on almost every page. Such antitheses are perhaps commonest at the conclusion either of speeches or of their natural subdivisions, but they are quite usual elsewhere. Occasionally they are heightened by assonance as in the lines quoted by Norden (408–9, cf. 314–15),

> γυναῖκες, ἐς μὲν ἐσθλ' ἀμηχανώταται,
> κακῶν δὲ πάντων τέκτονες σοφώταται.

Hence if, as seems inevitable, the structure and argumentation of such a debate as this of the *Medea* reflect the teachings of the early sophists, particularly Protagoras, then the style of the debate must do so equally. It may well be that in narrating a myth such as that ascribed to him by Plato (*Protag.* 320d–322a), Protagoras used the poetic and imagistic style that Aly conceives. Again, the fragment from his speech of condolence to Pericles (*Vorsokr.*[9] II, fg. 9, p. 268)— the passage most frequently cited as proof that Protagoras used only simple sentences heightened by poetic words—

proves merely that, like Antiphon the sophist,[67] he did not use antithesis in narratives. But that the man and the period which delighted in the juxtaposing of opposite ideas should not have carried that principle further and applied it to the structure of the sentence, particularly when we see Euripides doing exactly that, is incredible. After all, the greater antithesis of conflicting speeches and the lesser antithesis of balanced sentences spring from the same habit of thought and reflect the same desire, that of clarity enhanced by contrast.

But the *Medea* does not provide the earliest example of opposing speeches couched in antithetical language. Indeed, Drerup[68] could see in Euripides' less poetic idiom and longer sentences the marks of the periodic rather than of the earlier and truly antithetical style, and undoubtedly the technical skill of the debate in the *Medea* implies a period of development during which Euripides mastered the art of debate and imposed his own style on it. It is rather with the *Ajax* and the *Antigone* of Sophocles that the first complete ἀντιλογίαι appear, and these plays, the latter produced in 442 or 441 and the former almost certainly somewhat earlier, reveal very clearly the first stages in the art which was to enjoy so great a vogue as the century progressed. Doubtless, as Aly remarked,[69] the love of the ἀγών goes even further back to such contests as those between Homer and Hesiod, Calchas and Mopsus, Solon and Croesus. The ninth book of the *Iliad* shows arguments of a high order; and the *Eumenides* of Aeschylus embodies the conflict of two principles. And yet precisely because not even the conflict of the *Eumenides* achieves the clear and pointed expression of opposing speeches, does the emergence of

[67] See below, p. 105.
[68] "Theodoros von Byzanz," p. 229. Cf. Arist. *Rhet.* III 2.5.
[69] "Formprobleme," p. 98.

such speeches in the *Ajax* so clearly mark the beginning of a new era when the art of debate was for the first time seriously studied.

The play contains two debates, the one between Ajax and Tecmessa on the obligations of the εὐγενὴς ἀνήρ, the other between Teucer and Menelaus concerning the ultimate authority in the army at Troy. Both debates are highly symmetrical; in both the concluding lines so pointedly echo each other that, when actually heard, they must greatly have enhanced the effect of symmetry. As we have seen, Jason's and Medea's speeches likewise end with closely similar lines, and there can be no doubt that both playwrights consciously sought, and that the public had come to admire, this somewhat statuesque form of opposition. Thus, after Ajax has concluded (479–80),

> ἀλλ' ἢ καλῶς ζῆν ἢ καλῶς τεθνηκέναι
> τὸν εὐγενῆ χρή. πάντ' ἀκήκοας λόγον,

Tecmessa, after replying to his arguments and asking for pity, herself concludes (520–24),

> ἀνδρί τοι χρεὼν
> μνήμην προσεῖναι, τερπνὸν εἴ τί που πάθοι.
> χάρις χάριν γάρ ἐστιν ἡ τίκτουσ' ἀεί.
> ὅτου δ' ἀπορρεῖ μνῆστις εὖ πεπονθότος,
> οὐκ ἂν γένοιτ' ἔθ' οὗτος εὐγενὴς ἀνήρ.

Similarly the debate between Teucer and Menelaus, after the passionate opposition of the stichomythy, ends in two short symmetrical speeches each in the form of a riddle (1142–58).

But if the elaborate symmetry of these debates, remote as it is from anything in Aeschylus, strongly suggests the contemporary influence of Protagoras' ἀντιλογίαι, so does their content.[70] No one would, to be sure, maintain that the debates of the *Ajax* are abstract: Tecmessa's speech, for instance, owes much to the famous appeal of Andromache in the *Iliad* and, throughout, Sophocles seeks a dramatic, not a philosophic contrast. Yet the debates do embody general ideas. Unlike the speeches of the ninth *Iliad*, which concern purely concrete problems, these, as it were, lift the specific to the general, so that the immediate case comes to illustrate a widespread truth.[71] The matter is not easy to describe; indeed the debates of the *Ajax* illustrate only an early stage in this quality of abstraction, which is far better shown in the *Antigone*, the *Medea*, or the *Hippolytus*. And yet one can at least say that whereas Homer's generalizations almost entirely concern human beings—Odysseus in the ninth book, for instance, speaks as the skilled and realistic orator, Achilles as the impassioned youth, Phoenix as the sage elder, and thus like many of Homer's characters, they embody lasting human attitudes—in the *Ajax*, on the other hand, the first debate turns essentially on the abstract idea of εὐγένεια, the second on that of discipline.

Take for example the speech of Menelaus. After describing the outrages committed by Ajax (1052–62), he goes on to forbid his burial on the grounds that no state can survive without a hearty fear of authority, since fear alone holds an army together (1073–86),

> οὐ γάρ ποτ' οὔτ' ἂν ἐν πόλει νόμοι καλῶς
> φέροιντ' ἄν, ἔνθα μὴ καθεστήκῃ δέος,
> οὔτ' ἂν στρατός γε σωφρόνως ἄρχοιτ' ἔτι,
> μηδὲν φόβου πρόβλημα μηδ' αἰδοῦς ἔχων . . .

[70] Cf. Schmid-Stählin, I, 2, p. 490, "Mit diesen Wendungen ist schon das Gebiet der antithetischen Denkform betreten, die, bei Aischylos erst erwachend, durch Herakleitos, die Eleaten und besonders durch die rhetorischen Beleuchtungskünste der Sophistik vulgarisiert worden ist."

[71] *Ibid.*, p. 483, "so dass aus dem Kampf der augenblicklichen Interessen ein Kampf der Grundsätze zu werden scheint."

ἀλλ' ἐστάτω μοι καὶ δέος τι καίριον,
καὶ μὴ δοκῶμεν δρῶντες ἂν ἡδώμεθα
οὐκ ἀντιτείσειν αὖθις ἂν λυπώμεθα.

I have already discussed[72] the marked similarity of idea in this passage not only to the speech of Creon in the *Antigone* (esp. 661–80) but to those of Archidamus in Thucydides (I 80–85; II 11). There can, I think, be no doubt that Menelaus, pointedly referred to as a Spartan (1102), was intended to typify not merely the Spartan but, more widely, the oligarchic attitude. His references to Teucer's ill-birth, to the fact that he was a bowman rather than a hoplite (1120–23),[73] to the question whether Ajax came as an independent or a subordinate commander (1097–1101)—that issue, paramount since Salamis,[74] had not long since come to a head at Ithome—only strengthen the central impression of the lines already quoted. But if so, the similarities of thought between this passage and the speech of Archidamus have an added significance. The fact that in both a Spartan is made to expound in similar language the basic assumptions of the oligarchic state shows that Sophocles was already familiar with certain of those political generalizations which form the essence of Thucydides' speeches. Now Aly[75] saw the influence of Protagoras in the debate on constitutions of Herodotus III 80–82. The great sophist professed a knowledge of government (Plato *Protag.* 318e), and Aristoxenus found in his *Antilogies* the substance of Plato's *Republic*[76]— one thinks especially of Plato's discussion of the different forms of government. Certainly one would believe even without evidence that the rise of democratic Athens

[72] Above, chap. 1 pp. 14–17.
[73] Cf. Wilamowitz (*Herakles*² 1933) on *H. F.* 160, where Heracles is insulted for being a bowman.
[74] Thuc. I 91.7.
[75] "Formprobleme," p. 103.
[76] *Vorsokr.*⁹ II, fg. 5 (pp. 265–66).

stimulated widespread discussion of the contrary assumptions of democracy and oligarchy, but, as it is, the passages where the subject is actually discussed so markedly converge, as I have tried to show,[77] that one can only posit a considerable body of known political argument in the Periclean Age. And the first example of such argument, the more significant because like most of the later examples it appears in a debate, is this passage of the *Ajax*.

Thus, even in this earliest of his extant plays, Sophocles seeks in his debates a fundamental contrast of idea, and though his method is less abstract than that of Euripides who in the *Medea* opposes τὸ δίκαιον by τὸ συμφέρον and in the *Hippolytus* τὸ καλόν by the dictates of nature, yet basically it foreshadows these later debates. The *Antigone* seems to stand midway; for Creon there speaks in more general terms than Menelaus in setting forth much the same arguments (661–80), while Antigone by upholding the ἄγραπτοι νόμοι and the ties of family profoundly expresses the opposite position (450–57). Haemon and Creon likewise expound contrasting but equally general views on parental duty and the obligations of power (639–60, 684–739). In sum, if the later debates of Euripides and Thucydides, as Aly argues and as would doubtless be generally agreed, reflect the continuing influence of the ἀντιλογίαι of Protagoras, then it follows irresistibly that the debates of the *Ajax* and the *Antigone* betray the same influence at an earlier stage. For, although they are less developed than those of Euripides, and although Sophocles, unlike his rival, never was so fascinated by the abstract as to lose sight of purely human and personal motives, yet his debates introduce a method unknown to Aeschylus, in form and structure

[77] Above, chap. I pp. 14–17 (on oligarchy), pp. 21–25 (on democracy), where the relevant passages (besides those already cited, notably the tract of the Old Oligarch and Euripides' *Suppliants*) are discussed.

markedly resemble those of Euripides, anticipate ideas later used for similar contrasts by Thucydides, and in general, like the debates of both these authors, raise the purely personal conflict of situation to the higher conflict of idea. Certainly sophistic debate, if it taught anything, taught exactly this art of seeing the general implications of the specific act.

Thus by a somewhat circuitous route we return to the question of the antithetical style. As we saw, antithesis strongly marks the debate of the *Medea*, the finished skill of which seemed however to imply an earlier period when Euripides evolved not only his argumentation but, as Drerup contended, the more periodic tendencies of his style. If, therefore, the debates of the *Ajax* and the *Antigone* foreshadow those of the *Medea* and the *Hippolytus*, then their style should do so likewise. And that is in fact the case. The passage already cited from the *Ajax*, being antithetical throughout and closing with an elaborate homoioteleuton, is sufficient evidence from the earlier play, and for the *Antigone* one can perhaps do no better than refer to the exhaustive list by which Navarre supported his contention that Gorgias modeled his style on that of Sophocles.[78] There can, then, be no question that in this period when, I have argued, Sophocles deeply felt the influence of the sophistic debates, he also evolved an antithetical style by which to express them.

But one point of difference between the styles of the two plays may make the matter more clear and at the same time cast further doubt on Aly's contention that Protagoras' style, as well as that of Pericles, must have been primarily figurative and poetic. The difference is that, whereas the style of the *Ajax* is extremely figurative and becomes

[78] *Rhétorique Grecque*, pp. 102–9.

antithetical largely in the debates, the *Antigone*, though still figurative, stands out as easily the most tightly woven, the most antithetical of Sophocles' plays. In the former one thinks perhaps especially of the great figures drawn from the changes of nature by which Ajax justifies his own submission (670–76), but numerous others occur (8, 17, 140, 169–71, 196, 257, 582, 651, 1253–54), whereas in the *Antigone* the chief examples appear in Creon's tirade against Antigone (473–78, though also 712–17), where they are evidently intended as a contrast to her more measured speech. Now Sophocles, so Plutarch reports,[79] said that he affected three styles during his lifetime, first, the lofty style of Aeschylus, then an artificial style which he described as πικρὸν καὶ κατάτεχνον, and finally his most characteristic style, further qualified as ἠθικώτατον. One inevitably seeks to apply the statement to the marked changes in style between the *Ajax* and the *Antigone*. The former certainly cannot be in the second, so-called artificial manner, and its numerous figures and generally grandiose utterance seem to connect it with the first rather than with the third manner, though, on the other hand, it is definitely less Aeschylean than the fragments of the poet's earliest play, the *Triptolemus*. It may thus possibly illustrate the declining use of the first manner. The *Antigone*, on the other hand, from its very opening so consistently affects a balance and compression quite peculiar to itself—one thinks of such lines as (10),

πρὸς τοὺς φίλους στείχοντα τῶν ἐχθρῶν κακά

or (13–14),

δυοῖν ἀδελφοῖν ἐστερήθημεν δύο,
μιᾷ θανόντοιν ἡμέρᾳ διπλῇ χερί—

that it is difficult not to see in it an example of the second,

[79] Plut. *de Prof. in Virt.* 7, cf. Schmid-Stählin, I, 2, 313 n. 5.

83

artificial period.[80] But whether or not one accepts this interpretation, the fact remains that the *Antigone*, composed at a time when Protagoras enjoyed a great reputation in Athens and reflecting the antilogical mode of thought for which he was famous, is also in style the most antithetical not merely of Sophocles' but probably of all extant Greek tragedies. The fact cannot be a mere coincidence. Why should the poet have brusquely abandoned the great tradition of poetic language and why should he have sought the balance and intellectuality of prose, unless he was influenced by prose?

Finally, the decline in imagery between the *Ajax* and the *Antigone* and the increase in antithesis much weaken Aly's contention that not only Protagoras but Pericles sought their effects chiefly through imagery. Unquestionably Pericles used striking and memorable images such as the spring taken from the year, the Boeotians like old oaks breaking their limbs against each other, or war coming like a cloud from the Peloponnesus. But that was doubtless an immemorial usage known also to the old-fashioned Cimon, who called Athens and Sparta the yokefellows of Greece. Moreover, the practice continued with Antiphon and Gorgias, with whom poetic figures were by no means incompatible with the antithetical style. Now as we have seen, the debates of Sophocles and Euripides are expressed in an antithetical style, and since the debate as a form goes back to Protagoras, it has been argued that the style likewise did. Moreover, we have seen that Sophocles abandoned the grandeur of the *Ajax* for the logical, balanced manner of the *Antigone*, and again it was argued that the change is explic-

---

[80] So T. B. L. Webster (*Sophocles*, pp. 143–62), though he underestimates the differences between the styles of the *Ajax* and *Antigone* and hence ascribes both to the second period. On the other hand, K. Reinhardt (*Sophokles* [Frankfurt am Main 1933] 27) finds in the imagery of the *Ajax* a mark of Sophocles' early style.

able only by the increasing influence of prose. When, therefore, Aly conceives that Pericles in his actual Funeral Oration primarily relied on imagery and poetic diction, he is crediting him with fashions of speech quite abandoned by Euripides in the *Medea* of the same year, beginning to be abandoned even by Sophocles a decade earlier. Few would deny that tragedy was a living instrument, highly sensitive to the intellectual currents of the time. But if so, it clearly shows that the antithetical style attributed by Thucydides to Pericles would in fact have been familiar to him.

Since the argument, except as concerns Antiphon the sophist, is now complete, it remains only to summarize the chief points hitherto made. The tradition that Gorgias in the autumn of 427 first introduced at Athens not merely the so-called Gorgian figures but the antithetical style as such derives, it was seen, from Diodorus, who almost certainly quotes no more trustworthy a source than Timaeus and, moreover, wrote not as a serious critic of style but for the sweeping purposes of a universal history. Dionysius, though he regards the antithesis as Gorgian and can speak of Thucydides and Gorgias in one breath, expressly doubts the view upheld by Diodorus, and Cicero, possibly on the authority of Aristotle or Theophrastus, attributes antithesis to Thrasymachus, certainly in Athens before 427. Athenians of the fourth century seem to have been unaware of the importance of Gorgias' visit. Aristotle, who cites his style as best exemplifying the poeticisms of an earlier period of prose, is more interested in his use of set arguments and κοινοὶ τόποι, which he likewise attributes to Protagoras. Plato contents himself with parodying his mannered style in the speech of Agathon in the *Symposium*, the dramatic date of which is just before the Sicilian expedition, whereas in the *Protagoras*, imagined as taking place in the Periclean

Age, he ascribes a highly antithetical speech to Prodicus. Since Plato was careful to avoid anachronism, we may presumably take it as his opinion that the influence of Gorgias was not to be found in the antithetical style as such, which was used by earlier sophists, but in the artificial heightening of that style by means of the constant balance of clauses and by the equally constant rhyme and wordplay which were affected by the younger exquisites such as Agathon. Plato's view, it was argued, is confirmed not merely by the fragments of Agathon but by certain other considerations. First, the styles of Sophocles and Euripides, which shows no trace of the narrower Gorgian influence felt by Agathon, were evidently formed when antithesis was common, and are probably more antithetical in their early than in their late plays. Then, if the antithetical style was unknown in Athens before 427, the orator Antiphon must have changed his style with unprecedented speed not only in the *Tetralogies*, which were doubtless meant for students, but even in the speech on the Samothracian tribute, the unfamiliar mannerisms of which must then have shocked a jury of common men and thus have defeated their own ends. Again, Aristophanes in the Δαιταλῆς and Thucydides in the Mytilenean Debate speak of the rhetorical movement as widespread some months before Gorgias arrived, and to dissociate that movement from the antithetical style, particularly when it appears fully developed in Antiphon at or near the time and when Thucydides takes special pains to use it in the speech of Diodotus, truly requires an act of faith. Finally, in the *Acharnians*, produced a year and some months it is true after the arrival of Gorgias, Aristophanes describes the sentences then generally in vogue except among the older men as στρογγύλοι, the word used by Plato to describe the balanced sentences of Phaedrus' highly sophistic speech.

Among modern scholars, Blass, it was seen, and others concerned more narrowly with Thucydides accepted the antithetical style as Gorgian and accordingly called the historian's speeches, in style at least, anachronistic. Norden, on the other hand, largely moved by the evidence of tragedy, stated that the style was common among the sophists of the Periclean Age. Navarre, though he refused to dissociate early sophistry from rhetoric on the grounds that Athens was in close touch with the West after about 450, and though he amassed extremely full evidence on the antithetical style of the *Antigone*, lacked Norden's penetration when, instead of asking how Sophocles came to adopt that style, he tamely deduced that Sophocles was Gorgias' model. To Drerup falls the very great credit of fixing closely on the developed Gorgian traits of rhyme, wordplay, and consistent balance, and of stating that only their united presence suffices to prove Gorgian influence. Accordingly, he declared that mere antithesis was not Gorgian, even when, as in the *Tetralogies*, it is carried out with a certain rigor, but rather reflects the logical method and the search for precision and clarity which were introduced by the first generation of sophists.

Finally, Aly's detailed and in many ways penetrating study of early style gave rise to a fuller treatment of the evidence from tragedy. For, although Aly laid great weight on the dialogues and debates of Protagoras, particularly in their effect on Thucydides, he underestimated both the argumentation which they imply and their evident connection with the antithetical style. It was first pointed out that the use of εἰκότα and τεκμήρια appears in tragedy before the arrival of Gorgias; then, that the debates of the *Medea* and *Hippolytus* show a very advanced skill in contrasting the arguments from the just and the profitable, the noble and the natural. These same debates, it was seen, are not only symmetrical in outward form, but internally rely on clear and forceful antitheses, and both these traits, the outward and the inward, were found in the earlier *Ajax* and *Antigone*. Further, there seemed reason to believe that these debates of tragedy do in fact reflect the influence of the sophistic ἀντιλογίαι, particularly because they follow a recognized form differing from anything known to Aeschylus, and because at bottom they depend on those political and psychological generalizations which were in all probability given currency by the earliest sophists. Finally, it seemed more than a coincidence when Sophocles, in keeping with the spirit of contrast which pervades the *Antigone* and differentiates it from the earlier *Ajax*, also adopted an extremely antithetical style, which, it was suggested, is the style of his second period described by him as πικρὸν καὶ κατάτεχνον. In any case, the *Antigone* shows the declining importance of imagery in the tragic style and the great increase of antithesis. This fact, it seemed, could not be dissociated from the current fashions in argument and oratory, but rather encourages the belief that for a decade before the outbreak of the war, antithesis was, as Plato and Thucydides suggest, a common instrument of speakers.

III

These arguments then tend to discredit the view that Gorgias was, in the famous phrase, the only begetter of the antithetical style. By so doing, they likewise suggest that the speeches of Thucydides more faithfully echo the Athenian oratory which he knew before his exile than has commonly been thought. This is not the place to resume those larger questions which I attempted to discuss before—how far, for example, the accuracy of the speeches suffers through their numerous cross-references and pervading similarity of style[81] or, again, how a rhetoric perhaps appropriate to Athenians comports with Spartans or Corinthians[82] or, what is more important, whether we should think of fifth-century speakers as using arguments so profoundly general in character as those which appear in Thucydides[83]—in short, the larger questions concerning the nature and purpose of Thucydides' speeches. But even though these questions be left aside, still the fact, if granted, that not Gorgias but the sophists of the Periclean Age caused the widespread use of the antithetical style, would immensely enhance the essential truthfulness of the *History*, the more so since, as was said at the start, the thought both of Thucydides and of his speakers in many important ways demonstrably reflects that of the earlier period of which he writes. If, in other words, we could believe that, when at the beginning of the war, Thucydides first conceived the idea of his *History*, he inevitably conceived it in terms of the rationalism, the rhetorical method, and the style which were in the air about him, then it would be a matter of less importance for us to fix the exact proportion of fact and interpretation in the speeches (a task ultimately impossible in such complex works of art). For we should at least be able to say that, as a matter of historical fact, the great impulses shaping his thought and his style were felt by him in Athens, and that his book consequently reveals the Athenian mind as only something quite native can do. Then, though it were granted that through years of exile Thucydides achieved a greater pregnancy of style and a deeper abstraction of thought, still his book would in essence remain, not a mere interpretation of the past written in a style then unfamiliar, but a work

---

[81] Above, chap. I pp. 4–6, 52–53.
[82] Above, p. 36.   [83] Above, pp. 34–35, 52–53.

which in style as well as in thought carries the imprint of the past itself.

But the foregoing argument on the antithetical style, thus significant for our opinion of Thucydides, is seemingly confirmed by the fragments of the Περὶ Ὁμονοίας and Ἀλήθεια of Antiphon the sophist. The question here turns very largely on the dating of the two works, which Altwegg[84] and Aly,[85] against Jacoby[86] and Diels,[87] ascribed to the decade 440–430. If on examination the formers' views appear to have merit, then these fragments can by no means be neglected as evidence for the sophistic teachings of the Periclean Age. For though broken, they are considerably longer than any similar fragments from the same period, and though somewhat remote in subject matter from Thucydides and hence less pertinent to the *History* than more political works would have been, they would at least illustrate certain stylistic fashions current in the historian's early manhood. The further question, seemingly insoluble on the basis of our present knowledge, whether the sophist and the orator Antiphon are one person or two, does not affect our argument. It is perhaps enough to say that Xenophon (*Memor.* I 6), Plato (*Menex.* 236a), and Aristotle do not distinguish between them, though Xenophon includes traits[88] seemingly appropriate to the orator in a description which is generally taken to be of the sophist, and Aristotle cites now one, now the other, with the simple name Antiphon. Didymus[89] is the first person known to have distinguished between them, but whether

---

[84] *De Libro Περὶ Ὁμονοίας Scripto*, Basel 1908.
[85] "Formprobleme," p. 153.
[86] *De Antiphontis Sophistae Περὶ Ὁμονοίας Libro*, Berlin 1908.
[87] *Vorsokr.*⁹ II, pp. 357, n. 14; 359, n. 2.
[88] His φιλαργυρία, *Mem.* I 6.11, cf. the papyrus fg. of the Περὶ τῆς μετα-στάσεως (Gernet, *Antiphon*, p. 165), and Aly, "Formprobleme," p. 110.
[89] Cf. Hermogenes *de Id.* II 11.7, quoted below, p. 92.

he did so on good authority or merely because he assumed (as he might perhaps in his own time) that a serious forensic orator would not have composed the other more general works, is not known. A work on dreams, the purpose of which, as Aly (p. 100) argues on the basis of *de Divinatione*, II 144, was to give opposite and thus mutually destructive interpretations, was ascribed to the sophist, as was a Πολιτικός, the nature of which is unknown. Finally, if the Antiphon of Xenophon's portrait is in fact the sophist rather than the orator (the reverse could hardly be the case), then he is apparently as old as Socrates; if there is only one Antiphon, then his dates are those given for the orator, *ca*. 480–411.

Before considering the dates of the two works, it is worthwhile to observe two ancient criticisms of them. The first, on the Περὶ Ὁμονοίας, is from Philostratus (*V. Soph.* I 15.4), who remarks, speaking of Antiphon, λόγοι δ᾽ αὐτοῦ δικανικοὶ μὲν πλείους, ἐν οἷς ἡ δεινότης καὶ πᾶν τὸ ἐκ τέχνης ἔγκειται, σοφιστικοὶ δὲ καὶ ἕτεροι μέν, σοφιστικώτατος δὲ ὁ Ὑπὲρ τῆς ὁμονοίας, ἐν ᾧ γνωμολογίαι τε λαμπραὶ καὶ φιλόσοφοι σεμνή τε ἀπαγγελία καὶ ἐπηνθισμένη ποιητικοῖς ὀνόμασι καὶ τὰ ἀποτάδην ἑρμηνευόμενα παραπλήσια τῶν πεδίων τοῖς λείοις. Two traits, then, of the Περὶ Ὁμονοίας especially impressed Philostratus: the abundance of its γνῶμαι and the poeticisms of its language.

The other commentary is from Hermogenes (*de Ideis* II 11.7, p. 385 Walz), who, after saying that Didymus distinguished the orator from the author of the Πολιτικός and of the two works in question here, goes on to state his own doubts. On the one hand, he says, the two classes of works do differ in style; especially does the Ἀλήθεια differ from the rest. On the other hand, the ancient testimony (especially Plato's) does not suggest that there were two men, and though Thucydides is often said to have been the pupil of the orator from Rhamnus, yet τὸν μὲν Ῥαμνούσιον εἰδὼς ἐκεῖνον, οὗπερ εἰσὶν οἱ φονικοί, τὸν Θουκυδίδην δὲ πολλῷ κεχωρισμένον καὶ κεκοινωνηκότα τῷ εἴδει τῶν τῆς Ἀληθείας λόγων, πάλιν οὐ πείθομαι. Hermogenes reasons as follows: Thucydides is said to have been the pupil of Antiphon the orator, but his style more resembles that of the Ἀλήθεια than that of the orations, hence the orator must have composed the Ἀλήθεια. But, he remarks, since the styles of the two classes of works greatly differ, it may be assumed for purposes of exposition that there were two men, and he goes on to say of the sophist, ὁ δ' ἕτερος Ἀντιφῶν, οὗπερ οἱ τῆς Ἀληθείας εἰσὶ λεγόμενοι λόγοι, πολιτικὸς μὲν ἥκιστά ἐστι, σεμνὸς δὲ καὶ ὑπέρογκος τοῖς τε ἄλλοις καὶ τῷ δι' ἀποφάνσεων περαίνειν τὸ πᾶν, ὃ δὴ τοῦ ἀξιωματικοῦ τε λόγου ἐστὶ καὶ πρὸς μέγεθος ὁρῶντος, ὑψηλὸς δὲ τῇ λέξει καὶ τραχύς, ὥστε καὶ μὴ πόρρω σκληρότητος εἶναι. καὶ περιβάλλει δὲ χωρὶς εὐκρινείας, διὸ καὶ συγχεῖ τὸν λόγον καὶ ἔστιν ἀσαφὴς τὰ πολλά. καὶ ἐπιμελὴς δὲ κατὰ τὴν συνθήκην καὶ ταῖς παρισώσεσι χαίρων κτλ. ... The sophist Antiphon, then, deserts the language of ordinary life, seeking an impression of austerity through his constant generalizations and the roughness of his sounds. His diction is inclined to be unclear, and he is fond of balanced clauses, traits which are thought of as likewise conducing to his austerity.

We may now consider the dates of the two works, and first, that of the Περὶ Ὁμονοίας. The evidence consists almost wholly in its resemblances to certain passages of Sophocles and Euripides, perhaps the most striking of which appear in the long fg. 49.[90] The author is there expounding

---

[90] The references are to *Vorsokr.*⁹ II.

the difficulties of marriage: if it is unhappy, then to continue it is misery and to end it means the enmity of one's wife's family; if on the other hand it is happy, then to be responsible for another person is unbearable, when to be responsible for oneself is labor enough (οὐκ οὖν δῆλον, ὅτι γυνὴ ἀνδρί . . . οὐδὲν ἐλάττους τὰς φιλότητας παρέχεται καὶ τὰς ὀδύνας ἢ αὐτὸς αὑτῷ ὑπέρ τε τῆς ὑγιείας δισσῶν σωμάτων κτλ.). As evidence that Euripides knew this passage, Altwegg,[91] following Dümmler[92] and Nestle,[93] cited *Alcestis* 882–84,

> ζηλῶ δ' ἀγάμους ἀτέκνους τε βροτῶν·
> μία γὰρ ψυχή, τῆς ὑπεραλγεῖν
> μέτριον ἄχθος,

Hippolytus 258–59,

> τὸ δ' ὑπὲρ δισσῶν μίαν ὠδίνειν
> ψυχὴν χαλεπὸν βάρος,

also *Medea* 1090–1115, on the troubles of raising children (a passage which closely echoes the last lines of the fragment), and *Medea* 235–36, where the heroine says of marriage,

> κἂν τῷδ' ἀγὼν μέγιστος, ἢ κακὸν λαβεῖν
> ἢ χρηστόν,

to which one may compare from the present fragment μέγας γὰρ ἀγὼν γάμος ἀνθρώπῳ and the similar alternative that follows. Altwegg pointed to the exact parallel of ideas in the first and second of these passages, to the fact that the third is not a commonplace, since children are usually regarded as the protection and stay of their parents, and to the pervading similarity of structure in the fourth. It is true that Jacoby, who wrote independently on

[91] Pages 60–73; see above, n. 84.
[92] *Akademika*, p. 171.
[93] *Euripides*, p. 249.

the Περὶ Ὁμονοίας in the same year as Altwegg, refused to deduce that Euripides knew the sophist's work.[94] Yet he was able to cite from earlier poets only the statement that marriage can be a blessing or a curse,[95] and he failed to explain the closer similarities noted above. Diels, therefore, seems nearer the truth when he assumed borrowing on one part or the other,[96] though his conclusion that Antiphon was the borrower appears questionable for three reasons. First, when similar ideas are expressed consecutively by one author but in scattered passages by another, it is easy to see how the former could have influenced the latter but difficult to imagine the reverse. Then, the assumption that Euripides was the borrower is the more natural because he reverts to the ideas in question during the limited period from the *Alcestis* to the *Hippolytus*. One need not adduce instances to prove that one man may be influenced by another and lesser man whose ideas for a time fit his own, and then later, as his thought changes, escape that influence. Finally, Euripides seems to develop the ideas in his own and characteristic way. In the *Alcestis*, the view of marriage presented by Antiphon applies, as it does with him, to a man's life; in the *Medea*, to a woman's; in the *Hippolytus*, it concerns not marriage but the life of a nurse. But an essential similarity of expression remains throughout, as if Euripides had in mind a certain fixed series of thoughts which he then increasingly diverted to his own uses.

If these arguments hold, then the Περὶ Ὁμονοίας was written before the *Alcestis* of 438, and in fact it contains two parallels to the *Antigone*, the only other extant play of about the same period. The first, as has often been noted, is between fg. 61, ἀναρχίας δ᾽ οὐδὲν κάκιον ἀνθρώποις, and *Antigone*

Page 35; see above, n. 86.
Hes. *Theog.* 607, *Op.* 702; Semon. fg. 6.
*Vorsokr.*⁹ II, p. 357, n. to line 14.

672, ἀναρχίας δὲ μεῖζον οὐκ ἔστιν κακόν. But it has not commonly been observed that the contexts of both passages are closely similar. Just as Creon says that children should learn obedience that they may later become good soldiers who can endure the shock of battle, so Antiphon goes on, ταῦτα γινώσκοντες οἱ πρόσθεν ἄνθρωποι ἀπὸ τῆς ἀρχῆς εἴθιζον τοὺς παῖδας ἄρχεσθαι καὶ τὸ κελευόμενον ποιεῖν, ἵνα μὴ ἐξανδρούμενοι εἰς μεγάλην μεταβολὴν ἰόντες ἐκπλήσσοιντο. Then fg. 62, οἴῳ τις ἂν τὸ πλεῖστον τῆς ἡμέρας συνῇ, τοιοῦτον ἀνάγκη γενέσθαι καὶ αὐτὸν τοὺς τρόπους, echoes the thought of Ismene's lines (563–64),

οὐ γάρ ποτ', ὦναξ, οὐδ' ὃς ἂν βλάστῃ μένει
νοῦς τοῖς κακῶς πράσσουσιν, ἀλλ' ἐξίσταται.

The concept that a man's fortune and environment mold his character, first emphatically expressed by Simonides,[97] plays a large part in the thought of the fifth century, as Thucydides' account of the corruption of character through war and plague and Euripides' pervasive realism well show. The wording of Antiphon's passage is more closely echoed by a fragment of the *Phoenix* (fg. 812),

τοιοῦτός ἐστιν οἷσπερ ἥδεται ξυνών,

but its spirit appears clearly in the realism not merely of the *Telephus*, produced with the *Alcestis* in 438, but of the other plays on human wretchedness which Aristophanes ridicules in *Acharnians* 410–79. Now the whole trend of the Περὶ Ὁμονοίας was to portray life, in the words of fg. 51, as εὐκατηγόρητος ... καὶ οὐδὲν ἔχων περιττὸν οὐδὲ μέγα καὶ σεμνόν, ἀλλὰ πάντα σμικρὰ καὶ ἀσθενῆ καὶ ὀλιγο-χρόνια καὶ ἀναμεμειγμένα λύπαις μεγάλαις. And if these words suggest the sad quietism of Euripides' *Suppliants* (953) or of the conclusion of the *Heracles Mad*, they are certainly

[97] Fg. 4 (Diehl), 10–11, πράξας γὰρ εὖ πᾶς ἀνὴρ ἀγαθός, | κακὸς δ' εἰ κακῶς. Cf. C. M. Bowra, *Greek Lyric Poetry*, pp. 343–44, also chap. 1 above, p. 34.

as applicable to the earlier plays just noted; for, as we have seen, Aristophanes in 425 already thought of Euripides as portraying above all the commonness and smallness of existence. None of the parallels adduced in this paragraph necessarily points to the specific influence of the Περὶ Ὁμονοίας; indeed the reverse may rather be the case. But they at least show that this work of Antiphon deals with important and well-known ideas of the decade before the outbreak of the war, and by so doing, they confirm the date suggested by the more precise parallels of fg. 49.

There seems then no compelling reason why Jacoby[98] should have seen in the Περὶ Ὁμονοίας merely a panacea for the discords of Greece which Thucydides describes in III 82–83. It is true that Kramer's[99] later dissertation, by showing that the word ὁμόνοια was commonly used in a civic context, tended to confirm Jacoby's social interpretation of the work against Altwegg's view that it wholly concerned the individual's agreement with himself. Yet the extant fragments, as well as the description in Iamblichus,[100] amply prove that Antiphon at least emphasized the individual rather than the state, and no one who has in mind the purely personal problems of love or misfortune which Euripides treated in the thirties can say that such an emphasis is unthinkable at that time. On the contrary, the peaceful years before 431 doubtless left men freer to ponder on the new individualism fostered by the sophists than did the following period of civic and factional heat. Finally, the parallels between Democritus[101] and the Περὶ Ὁμονοίας prove nothing in regard to the date of the latter; for it is not known in what work or when Democritus discussed the

[98] Pages 9–11; see above, n. 86.
[99] *Quid Valeat ὁμόνοια in Litteris Graecis*, Göttingen 1915.
[100] *Vorsokr.*9 II, fg. 44a (p. 356).
[101] Fgs. 200, 227, 250, 255, 276.

subject of concord. That his teachings as a whole were far
more systematic than Antiphon's and that his remarks on
ὁμόνοια (esp. fgs. 250 and 255) appear to have been more
social in their implication, may suggest that Democritus
was the later. In sum, it is difficult to escape Altwegg's
conclusion, accepted categorically by Aly, that the Περὶ
Ὁμονοίας was composed shortly after 440. Certainly it
contains sufficiently close and sufficiently numerous parallels
to the works of roughly the same period to cast the burden
of proof on those who dispute the dating.

The three papyrus fragments of the Ἀλήθεια, the first
two of which were published in 1915 by Grenfell and Hunt
and the third in 1922,[102] were unknown to Altwegg and
Jacoby, and it has remained principally for Aly[103] to consider the date of the work of which they form part of the
second book. On several grounds he ascribes it to the end
of the decade 440–430. In the first place, its title reflects the
spirit of Parmenides and Protagoras, the former of whom
expounded Ἀληθείης εὐκυκλέος ἀτρεμὲς ἦτορ (1.29–30),
while the latter wrote an Ἀλήθεια ἢ καταβάλλοντες. The
descending line of influence thus suggested Aly[104] brilliantly
confirmed by an analysis of the mathematical proofs known
to the three men. It is unnecessary to restate his argument
here: in essence, it is that Antiphon in the first book of the
Ἀλήθεια (fg. 13) applied to the problem of squaring the
circle the Eleatic idea of infinite divisibility which Zeno,
Protagoras, and Anaxagoras knew in a more general and
philosophic sense, but that Democritus, on the other hand,
not only repudiated the general idea in his atomic theory
but specifically rejected its use in the problem to which

[102] *Vorskr.*⁹ II, fg. 44 (pp. 346–55).
[103] "Formprobleme," pp. 115–56.
[104] *Ibid.*, pp. 115–16, 141–47.

Antiphon had applied it;[105] finally, that Hippias[106] approached the same problem by a more developed solution apparently unknown to Antiphon. On this view, then, Antiphon would stand after Zeno and Protagoras and feel their influence more strongly than did Hippias, while on the other hand he would definitely precede Democritus, a point which confirms what was suggested of their relationship in the last paragraph. The fact that Anaxagoras, while in prison in 433 on the motion of Diopeithes,[107] is said to have diverted himself with the same problem (by what solution is not known), indicates, as Aly says, the period when it had come to be of interest.

Then, Aly[108] seeks a second indication of date in the argument of the papyrus fragments themselves on the relative authority of φύσις and νόμος. It is his general purpose to distinguish an earlier period, when the difference between local and universal law first became apparent, from a later period when that difference was used to justify such doctrines of might as Plato attributes to Callicles and Thrasymachus, and Thucydides to the generals at Melos. For certainly no such doctrines appear in the Ἀλήθεια, which, as another critic has justly said,[109] merely argues that an individual, whether he wishes or not, must logically prefer the consistent dictates of natural law to the follies and inconsistencies of civic law. Though he presents such an individualism as inevitable, Antiphon apparently does not consider it widespread; much less does he advocate the unrestrained individualism which springs from the contempt of civic law. When, therefore, Aly goes on to ascribe this

[105] Fg. 155. Aly, p. 115.
[106] Fg. 21. Aly, pp. 144–46.
[107] Plut. *de Exil.* 17; *Per.* 32. On the date of Anaxagoras' expulsion, cf. H. T. Wade-Gery, "Thucydides the Son of Melesias," *JHS* 52 (1932) 220.
[108] Pages 117–33.
[109] F. Altheim, *Klio* 20 (1926) 257–70.

later unrestrained individualism to the years after the Peace of Nicias and to argue that the 'Αλήθεια must therefore be sensibly earlier, he seems to have much right on his side, the more so since the distinction between local and universal law was well known to the Periclean Age, as is clear from Empedocles fg. 135, *Antigone* 454, Herodotus III 38, and the tradition in Suidas that Archelaus [110] expounded the doctrine. Both Plato (*Protag.* 337c) and Xenophon (*Mem.* IV 4) cause Hippias to talk of φύσις and νόμος, but, as Aly remarks, his reputation for encyclopedic learning suggests that he adopted rather than originated the idea. Aly (p. 133) attributes its widespread currency to Protagoras, and with great likelihood; but however that may be, it is at least certain that by the time of the *Antigone* the doctrine was already well known.

Finally the 'Αλήθεια, like the Περὶ 'Ομονοίας, contains resemblances to the early plays of Sophocles and Euripides. Perhaps the most striking appears in the *Hippolytus* where Phaedra, after describing her futile struggle to quench her love, concludes (403–4)

> ἐμοὶ γὰρ εἴη μήτε λανθάνειν καλὰ
> μήτ' αἰσχρὰ δρώσῃ μάρτυρας πολλοὺς ἔχειν.

Just so, in the opening lines of the first papyrus fragment,[111] Antiphon says that a man will succeed best, εἰ μετὰ μὲν μαρτύρων τοὺς νόμους μεγά⟨λο⟩υς ἄγοι, μονούμενος δὲ μαρτύρων τὰ τῆς φύσεως. For, he continues, transgressions of civic law are punished only when they are known, but transgressions of the law of nature entail their own automatic punishment[112]—τὰ οὖν νόμιμα παραβαίνων εἰὰν λάθῃ τοὺς ὁμολογήσαντας, καὶ αἰσχύνης καὶ ζημίας

[110] *Vorsokr.*9 II, A2 (p. 45).
[111] Col. 1.16–23 (*Vorsokr.*9 II, p. 346).
[112] Col. 2.3–20.

ἀπήλλακται· μὴ λαθὼν δ' οὔ. τῶν δὲ τῇ φύσει ξυμφύτων ἐάν τι παρὰ τὸ δυνατὸν βιάζηται, ἐάν τε πάντας ἀνθρώπους λάθῃ, οὐδὲν ἔλαττον τὸ κακόν, ἐάν τε πάντες ἴδωσιν, οὐδὲν μεῖζον. Now, as was observed,[113] the debate between Phaedra and the nurse, like the Mytilenean Debate in Thucydides, turns on the opposite concepts of legal right and inescapable natural force. When, therefore, the nurse, in opposing Phaedra's honorable desire to die, adduces the overwhelming power of Aphrodite (438–58), whose shameful commands, she says, men perforce must obey,

$$ἐν \ σοφοῖσι \ γὰρ$$
$$τάδ' \ ἐστὶ \ θνητῶν, \ λανθάνειν \ τὰ \ μὴ \ καλά \ (465\text{-}66),$$

she clearly expounds the same doctrine of natural law as Antiphon and echoes his precept of secrecy. Fragments of the earlier *Hippolytus* (fgs. 433, 434) and of the *Bellerophon* (fg. 286) repeat the idea. The next resemblance is found in the *Medea*,[114] where Creon twice states that a man must anticipate his enemies by vigorous action and not let αἰδώς interfere with policy. In the same way, Antiphon confirms his argument by citing as an example of those who harm themselves by following conventional rather than natural law,[115] ⟨οἵτινε⟩ς ἂν παθόντες ἀμύνωνται καὶ μὴ αὐτοὶ ⟨ἄρχ⟩ωσι τοῦ δρᾶν. It is significant that Thucydides attributes this same realistic outlook to the Corcyreans in 433 (I 33.4).[116] The debates of the *Medea* and *Hippolytus*, as has already been said, are permeated with the influence of the sophists, and it would hardly be denied that that influence shows itself as much in a deeper rationalism of outlook as in a more conscious rhetorical skill—indeed the two are

---

[113] Above, n. 66.
[114] Lines 289–91, 349 (αἰδούμενος δὲ πολλὰ δὴ διέφθορα).
[115] Fg. A, col. 4.32–col. 5.3.
[116] Cf. above, chap. I pp. 12–13.

merely facets of the same influence. When then these plays present close resemblances to one fragment of the ᾽Αλήθεια, brief as it is, it is difficult not to see in it an example of the sophistic writings which those plays reflect.

Other indications of the same fact exist. For instance, Aly[117] with some probability saw in the words[118] οὐ γὰρ διὰ δόξαν βλάπτεται, ἀλλὰ δι᾽ ἀλήθειαν the contrast between truth and opinion which played an important part in the teachings of Parmenides (1.29) and probably of Protagoras.[119] Again, the suggestion of fg. B that it is the mark of barbarians to revere high birth echoes the judgment of Περὶ ᾽Αέρων ῾Υδάτων Τόπων (ch. XVI) and of Herodotus, while the following argument that all men are in fact equal seems inspired by the same enthusiasm for sweeping scientific truths which marks the former of the two works just cited. Then, the doctrine that it is against nature to respect your parents if they are bad seems just such a sophistic tenet as would prompt Aristophanes to say that all pupils of the sophists beat their parents (*Vesp.* 1038, *Nub.* 1338–41, 1420–29). He makes Pheidippides justify the doctrine in Antiphon's way as a law of nature (1427–29), and is again at one with him (fg. 25) in speaking of Δῖνος (380), though certainly Anaxagoras and Diogenes propounded the idea, which Antiphon doubtless merely utilized in his first book. Since Aristophanes must necessarily have travestied only the better known and therefore longer standing sophistic tenets, the doctrines just spoken of were presumably familiar sometime before the *Wasps* and the *Clouds*. In general, it can be said that Aristophanes' portrait of a sophist as partly absorbed in the physical sciences and partly given to novel and subversive ideas on human

[117] Page 115.
[118] Fg. A, col. 2.21–23.
[119] Plato *Theaet.* 166d.

relations is admirably exemplified in the 'Aλήθεια, the first
book of which treated the external world and the second,
human society. Finally, it may not be farfetched to see in
the 'Aλήθεια a certain kinship to the *Antigone*. Both authors
contrast universal with local laws, though the pious
Sophocles finds in the former a religious, not a natural,
force. In Creon's speech to Haemon on a child's duties to
his parents (639–47) Sophocles again touches a question
which, as we have seen, was treated by the sophist, though
again the emphasis of the two works is quite different.
Lastly, when Creon says to Antigone that in honoring
Polynices she dishonors Eteocles (512–22), he states the
dilemma of the third fragment which Antiphon sums up by
saying,[120] τὸ γὰρ ⟨ἄ⟩λλους ὠφελοῦν ἄλ⟨λο⟩υς βλάπτει.
Since Antiphon is illustrating the inconsistencies of civic
law, his use of the idea is again different from that of
Sophocles, whose nobility of attitude is nowhere better
shown than in Antigone's reply that death cancels such
inconsistencies. It need hardly be said that there is no question
here of direct influence, but when the *Antigone* as a whole
expounds a great philosophic problem with a kind of bare
clarity unknown to earlier verse and at the same time
canvasses certain of the minor problems which appear in
the 'Aλήθεια, it is perhaps not too fanciful to believe that
the vision of Sophocles, like his style, was then being
sharpened by the discussions of the first sophists. It would
take us far afield to consider whether, in maintaining the
sanctity of strong character and the awful but ultimately
beneficent power of the gods, Sophocles was in fact opposing
an opportunism and an agnosticism which he felt in the
sophistic teachings about him. But the fact at least that, in
however different a spirit, he yet treats certain of the same

[120] Col. 2.30–32.

questions as Antiphon, suggests something concerning the period when those questions were of interest in Athens.

Thus, although absolute certainty cannot result from such discussions as the foregoing, the strong probability must remain that the Ἀλήθεια was written some time near or just before the outbreak of the war, perhaps, as Aly suggests,[121] a few years later than the Περὶ Ὁμονοίας. Certainly, if both were written considerably later, they would apparently have concerned ideas already somewhat commonplace, an assumption hardly just to their evident seriousness. But if so much be granted, then we may return to the main question of the essay and consider what light is cast by these works on the stylistic fashions of pre-Gorgian Athens. For that purpose the foregoing discussion was perhaps not strictly necessary; for even Jacoby,[122] though he regarded the Περὶ Ὁμονοίας as somewhat later than did Altwegg, agreed that it was written during the early years of the war, a date likewise assumed by Altheim[123] for the Ἀλήθεια. Hence, on any current view the two works might naturally be thought to reflect many stylistic elements of the years before 427. Yet so great has been the magic of Gorgias' name, that it seemed best to set forth somewhat fully the arguments in the case, which in fact tend to support the earlier date. For only by so doing can one transcend the inveterate habit of seeing in the antitheses of early Athenian prose the influence of Gorgias and of Gorgias alone.

It is unnecessary to analyze the style of the Περὶ Ὁμονοίας in great detail since Jacoby[124] has already done so. As Aly observed,[125] the work is apparently a sophistic epideixis, and as such it may be expected to reveal a poetic

[121] Page 153.
[122] Pages 10–11, 35; see above, n. 86.
[123] See above, n. 109.
[124] Pages 48–69; see above, n. 86. [125] Page 154.

cast of speech and an abundance of γνῶμαι foreign to the more scientific Ἀλήθεια. Jacoby noted its use of the old-Attic ξύν,[126] of the Ionic -σσ-, of poetic and Ionic words presumably uncommon in normal speech, of words with unusual meanings (it is suggestive that Harpocration often cites from the Περὶ Ὁμονοίας[127]), and of compound words. Significant as these traits are in connection with the language of Thucydides, more significant is the author's marked preference of nouns to verbs. Thus he uses such a phrase as ὑπὲρ τοῦ καθ᾽ ἡμέραν βίου ἐς τὴν ξυλλογήν[128] or μεγάλων πόνων . . . εἰς ἀνάγκας.[129] Similarly, he often makes an abstract noun subject of the sentence (αἱ γὰρ ἡδοναὶ οὐκ ἐπὶ σφῶν αὐτῶν ἐμπορεύονται[130]), uses neuter adjectives in a general sense(ἐν τῷ αὐτῷ δέ γε τούτῳ, ἔνθα τὸ ἡδύ, ἔνεστι πλησίον που καὶ τὸ λυπηρόν[131]), and articular infinitives (καὶ ἐν μὲν τῷ γεγενῆσθαι οὐκ ἔνεστιν, ἐν δὲ τῷ μέλλειν ἐνδέχεται ⟨καὶ τὸ μὴ⟩ γενέσθαι[132]).

This last example leads on to the structure of his sentences which Jacoby[133] summed up by saying, "Nimirum scriptor parallelismum sententiarum adeo excoluit, ut quasi stropham antistropha excipiat." Antiphon commonly connects his sentences, it is true, by repeating a word from one sentence in the next, a practice more reminiscent of Protagoras' looser style (cf. fgs. 4 and 9) than of the compression of Thucydides. Moreover, he often uses such lists of nouns as appear in the

[126] On these usages in early Attic, cf. B. Rosencranz, "Der lokale Grundton und die persönliche Eigenart in der Sprache des Thukydides und der älteren attischen Redner," *Indoger. Forsch.* 48 (1930) 127–78.
[127] Cf. fgs. 67–71.
[128] Fg. 49, *Vorsokr.*⁹ II, p. 359.6.
[129] *Ibid.*, p. 359.2.
[130] *Ibid.*, p. 358.9–10.
[131] *Ibid.*, p. 358.8–9.
[132] Fg. 58, *ibid.*, p. 363.18.
[133] Page 65; see above, n. 86.

second fragment of Protagoras just cited. Nevertheless, his style, except in passages of narrative (an exception equally true for Thucydides and Antiphon the orator), is unquestionably based on antithesis and parallelism, the more markedly so, the more abstract and gnomic his thought. A good example is fg. 54, where Antiphon in simple, fluent sentences tells a fable on the use of money. When he sums it up, his style becomes more balanced,[134] ὅτῳ γάρ τις μὴ ἐχρήσατο μηδὲ χρήσεται, ὄντος ἢ μὴ ὄντος αὐτῷ οὐδὲν οὔτε πλέον οὔτε ἔλασσον βλάπτεται. When he adds a general reflection, he falls into truly antithetical clauses, ὅτῳ γὰρ ὁ θεὸς μὴ παντελῶς βούλεται ἀγαθὰ διδόναι ἀνδρί, χρημάτων πλοῦτον παρασχών, τοῦ καλῶς φρονεῖν ⟨δὲ⟩ πένητα ποιήσας, τὸ ἕτερον ἀφελόμενος ἀμφοτέρων ἀπεστέρησεν. Again in fg. 58 one sees how naturally the abstraction of a γνώμη is clarified and made precise by antithesis[135]— ἐλπίδες δ' οὐ πανταχοῦ ἀγαθόν· πολλοὺς γὰρ τοιαῦται ἐλπίδες κατέβαλον εἰς ἀνηκέστους συμφοράς, ἃ δ' ἐδόκουν τοῖς πέλας ποιήσειν, παθόντες ταῦτα ἀνεφάνησαν αὐτοί. Jacoby[136] accordingly rejected Blass's statement that the Gorgian figures were absent from the Περὶ Ὁμονοίας by adducing, in addition to the sentences just quoted, such other examples as fg. 49,[137] δοκοῦντα ἡδονὰς κτᾶσθαι λύπας ἄγεσθαι, and, from the same passage, ἴσα φρονοῦντας ἴσα πνέοντας, ἀξιώσαντα καὶ ἀξιωθέντα. Yet Blass's view is undoubtedly correct in the sense that the more precise Gorgian traits of the *Helen*, that is, its short balanced clauses, its punning, wordplay, and rhyme, are foreign to this work. But if so, one is again led to the conclusion of the previous section, that antithesis, occasionally heightened by παρίσωσις and παρομοίωσις, is not in itself Gorgian but, rather,

134 *Vorsokr.*9 II, p. 362.12–14.
135 Ibid., p. 364.3–6.
136 Page 58; as above, n. 86.
137 *Vorsokr.*9 II, p. 358.4–5.

characteristic of an earlier sophistic prose already wide-spread before 427. It was also argued that, being in essence merely an aid to clarity particularly helpful in abstractions, antithesis must have been used by Protagoras in the debates the influence of which is seen in the early plays of Sophocles and Euripides. Certainly, the fact that Antiphon, revealing as he does certain of the same stylistic traits as Protagoras, uses antithesis for exactly that purpose must seem to confirm such an assumption.

Aly [138] has called the *'Aλήθεια* an *ὑπόμνημα* or scientific essay, similar in kind to the *Περὶ 'Αρχαίης 'Ιητρικῆς* and perhaps, as has recently been argued, [139] to the tract of the Old Oligarch. In style and feeling it shows little of the exuberance of the *Περὶ 'Ομονοίας* but approaches rather, as Hermogenes suggests, if not the speeches of Thucydides, at least such reasoned expository passages as the Archaeology or the description of *στάσις* (III 82–83). Like the *Περὶ 'Ομονοίας*, it uses the old-Attic *ξύν* but, unlike it, at times the old-Attic *-ττ-*. Its language is not generally poetic or imaginative, but it perhaps even surpasses the other work in its preference for substantives. For example, in the passage [140] εἰ μὲν οὖν τις τοῖς τοιαῦτα προσ⟨ι⟩εμένοις ἐπικούρησις ἐγίγνετο παρὰ τῶν νόμων, τοῖς δὲ μὴ προσιεμένοις ἀλλ' ἐναντιουμένοις ἐλάττωσις, οὐκ ἀν⟨όνητον ἂν⟩ ἦν τ⟨ὸ τοῖς νό⟩μοις πεῖ⟨σμα. νῦν⟩ δὲ φαίνε⟨ται τοῖς⟩ προσιεμ⟨ένοις⟩ τὰ τοιαῦτα τὸ ἐ⟨κ⟩ νόμου δίκαιον οὐχ ἱκανὸν ἐπικουρεῖν, the author three times uses an abstract noun in the nominative and once a neuter adjective. Similarly, he has constant recourse to abstract neuter plurals and the articular infinitive. But what most concerns ourselves is the marked symmetry

---

[138] Page 155.
[139] K. I. Gelzer, "Die Schrift vom Staate der Athener," *Hermes*, Einzelschriften 3 (1937) 93.
[140] Fg. A, col. 5.25–col. 6.9.

of his clauses. As in the Περὶ Ὁμονοίας, he sometimes makes his transitions by repeating words and he occasionally gives lists,[141] but on the whole, his method is to make a statement and then to analyze it in a series of contrasting clauses which, it must be agreed, admirably clarify his somewhat complex train of thought. The opening lines of fg. A well illustrate his method: δικαιοσύνη ⟨οὖ⟩ν τὰ τῆς πό⟨λεω⟩ς νόμιμα ⟨ἐν⟩ ᾗ ἂν πολιτεύηταί τις, μὴ ⟨παρ⟩αβαίνειν. χρῷτ᾽ ἂν οὖν ἄνθρωπος μάλιστα[θ] ἑαυτῷ ξυμφερόντως δικαιοσύνῃ, εἰ μετὰ μὲν μαρτύρων τοὺς νόμους μεγά⟨λο⟩υς ἄγοι, μονούμενος δὲ μαρτύρων τὰ τῆς φύσεως· τὰ μὲν γὰρ τῶν νόμων ⟨ἐπίθ⟩ετα, τὰ δὲ ⟨τῆς⟩ φύσεως ἀ⟨ναγ⟩καῖα· καὶ τὰ ⟨μὲν⟩ τῶν νόμων ὁμολογη⟨θέντ⟩α οὐ φύν⟨τ᾽ ἐστί⟩ν, τὰ δὲ ⟨τῆς φύσ⟩εως φύν⟨τα οὐχ⟩ ὁμολογηθέντα.[142] Or again, one may quote,[143] καὶ τούτων τῶν εἰρημένων πόλλ᾽ ἄν τις εὕροι πολέμια τῇ φύσει· ἔνι τ᾽ ἐν αὑτοῖς [δ᾽] ἀλγύνεσθαί τε μᾶλλον, ἐξὸν ἥττω[ι], καὶ ἐλάττω ἥδεσθαι, ἐξὸν πλείω, καὶ κακῶς πάσχειν, ἐξὸν μὴ πάσχειν. In these two typical passages the author's constant reliance on short antithetical clauses needs no comment, but it is worth observing that he is thus led to emphasize single words with that starkness which has often been observed in the style of Thucydides or of the *Tetralogies*. Again, though his thought often falls into completely balanced clauses, such symmetry seems to be less a mannerism with him than an inevitable result partly of his struggle for clarity, partly of the similar sounds and number of syllables in the Greek endings. For, like Thucydides and unlike Gorgias, he at other times neglects perfect symmetry, as if he valued it not for itself but for its usefulness. And if in this respect his style differs from that of Gorgias, so in a

[141] Cf. fg. A, col. 2.30–col. 3.18.
[142] The author continues with the longer passage quoted above, pp. 99–100.
[143] Fg. A, col. 5.13–24, continued by the passage quoted on p. 106 above.

larger sense does the nature of the tract itself. We have little reason to believe that Gorgias often wrote on speculative and scientific subjects; even his Περὶ τοῦ μὴ ὄντος has been regarded as both early and essentially light.[144] Rather, one seems to see in the 'Αλήθεια the same rationalistic spirit of such a work as Protagoras' 'Αλήθεια ἢ καταβάλλοντες, the first sentence of which has already been cited[145] as an example of this same (as one might call it) clarifying use of antithesis. If so, then this work of Antiphon, as the indications of its date suggest, must seem to derive in style as well as in spirit from the earlier sophistic movement which antedated the arrival of Gorgias in Athens by some twenty years.

Thus the argument of this section, except for one concluding point, is at an end. It has been impossible, it is true, to discuss in detail the very real resemblances of thought or language between Antiphon and Thucydides or to analyze the latter's style for resemblances other than those briefly suggested in passing. But such an analysis, even if it had been attempted, would not perhaps have yielded the fullest evidence, especially in regard to the speeches, because these two works of Antiphon, the one probably an epideixis and the other an ὑπόμνημα, differ in kind from any speech of Thucydides. It would perhaps be fair to say that the style of a public oration would stand somewhere between the exuberant sententiousness of the former and the cool logic of the latter, and would thus mitigate the divergent extremes of each. The aforementioned debates of tragedy, for instance, reveal in the clarity of their argumentation something of the logical spirit and antithetical method of the ὑπόμνημα, while at the same time their language is far more varied and their movement less intense. Now, as I

---

[144] H. Gomperz, *Sophistik und Rhetorik* (Leipzig 1912) 1-35.
[145] Page 70.

have tried to show,[146] we have no reason to believe that the oratory of the latter half of the fifth century was specific in content, and concerned, like the speeches of Lysias or most modern oratory, with separate and unique circumstances. Rather, the very arguments from what is likely or profitable or just and the practice both of the tragedians and of Thucydides suggest that men were then primarily concerned with classes of events and the broader aspects of thought, in the light of which they considered specific events. In other words, a peculiar mark of fifth-century thought was its capacity for general ideas, a capacity by no means unnatural even to uneducated audiences in times of great change and opportunity, as the sermons of early Protestantism and the writings of the French and American revolutions clearly show. But if in its manner of reasoning and its concern with broad generalizations, public oratory thus probably did not greatly differ from the debates of tragedy or from these tracts of Antiphon, then it is hard to believe that the antithetical style, which in both these classes of works is merely the vehicle of abstract thought, was unknown to oratory. On the contrary, considering the unity and alertness of Athenian life, we must rather believe that oratory revealed the stylistic and intellectual influences of the early sophists as much as any other class of writings, perhaps more than any other, since the sophists were from the first teachers of oratory. Thus it must appear natural that even the speeches of Thucydides' first books should abound in generalizations couched in antitheses.

This conclusion leads to a final point concerning the remoter origins of the antithetical style. Diels,[147] believing

---

[146] Above, chap. 1 pp. 34-35, 52-53. Cf. A. Croiset, *Thucydide*, p. 101, "de là l'obligation d'aller chaque fois au fond des choses et d'épuiser, pour ainsi dire, la théorie du sujet en question. Ce charactère tient aussi au temps: l'éloquence devait alors être abstraite, parce que les idées générales n'avaient pas encore été formulées."

[147] "Gorgias und Empedokles," *Sitzungsber. d. Berl. Akad.* (1844) 343-68.

that Gorgias discovered antithetical prose, sought his model in the verse of Empedocles; Norden, as has been said, sought it in the sentences of Heraclitus, and Navarre in the early tragedies of Sophocles, though, as they agreed, Greek from the first readily lent itself to such effects of balance and contrast. Now in perhaps no part of early literature are these effects more marked than in the γνῶμαι of Homer and especially of Theognis. The hexameter readily expressed antithesis in such lines as

οὐκ ἀγαθὸν πολυκοιρανίη· εἷς κοίρανος ἔστω (B 204)

or αἰδομένων ἀνδρῶν πλέονες σάοι ἠὲ πέφανται,
φευγόντων δ' οὔτ' ἄρ κλέος ὄρνυται οὔτε τις ἀλκή
(E 531–32).

Even more so did the pentameter, in which the pause at the middle of the line seems naturally to induce a balance of expression. One could cite many such lines from the elegists as these of Theognis and Solon,

οὔτε γὰρ ἂν πόντον σπείρων βαθὺ λήιον ἀμῷς
οὔτε κακοὺς εὖ δρῶν εὖ πάλιν ἀντιλάβοις
(Theogn. 107–8)

or χρήματα μὲν δαίμων καὶ παγκάκῳ ἀνδρὶ δίδωσιν,
Κύρν'· ἀρετῆς δ' ὀλίγοις ἀνδράσι μοῖρ' ἕπεται
(Theogn. 149–50)

or εἶναι δὲ γλυκὺν ὧδε φίλοισ', ἐχθροῖσι δὲ πικρόν,
τοῖσι μὲν αἰδοῖον, τοῖσι δὲ δεινὸν ἰδεῖν
(Solon 1.5–6).

Now, as was argued in the last paragraph, the oratory of the fifth century was undoubtedly much given to generalization. Certainly it could not be denied that the speeches of Thucydides, the debates of tragedy, and the fragments of the sophist Antiphon contain many abstract and general passages and that in these passages antithesis is most marked.

Thus, in the new edition of his *Geschichte der griechischen Literatur* (I, 2, 483), Schmid could describe the style of Sophocles as gnomic, though at the same time it is antithetical. Hence, rather than follow Diels, Norden, or Navarre in seeking the model of the antithetical style in one or another author, it would seem more natural to suppose that, partly through the native logic of their tongue and partly for clarity's sake, the Greeks from the first associated antithesis with those generalizations which were renewed from age to age in the form of γνῶμαι. Then when, after the middle of the fifth century, prose increasingly supplanted verse as the vehicle of serious thought, it in turn fell heir to the older tradition of gnomic antithesis and carried it further, both because the tradition was firmly established and because the generalizations of prose were more complex and hence more in need of analysis. Thus, though the early sophists evolved their sententious and antithetical style to emulate the dignity of gnomic verse, prose soon so surpassed its model in balance and trenchancy, that Sophocles and Euripides, in curtailing the chorus in favor of debates and orations more in keeping with the rational spirit of their age, at the same time affected a more balanced and sententious style than had been used by earlier poets. It is this style that inspired the fragments of the sophist Antiphon and, so it has been argued, the oratory known to Thucydides at the outbreak of the war and later taken by him as the basis of the speeches in his *History*. Gorgias' part in the development of the style seems therefore much less great than has been supposed. It is possible that he evolved his strict antithetical manner in Sicily some years before 427 and that other sophists carried his teachings to Athens before he actually came. It is more probable that he neither discovered the antithetical style nor brought it into general use, but merely pressed it, so to speak, to its illogical conclusion, seeking in every detail and by every means a symmetry and balance of expression which his predecessors had used with greater moderation and largely for the sake of clarity.

IV

A few words should be added in summary and in apology: in summary, because the foregoing argument has necessarily often strayed from the original question, how far Thucydides' style is representative of his age, and it will therefore be useful to return briefly to the subject in conclusion; in apology, because, as Dr. Jan Ros[148] has made clear, the traits of symmetry and balance have doubtless been over-emphasized. Dr. Ros pointed out that Thucydides' style relies on three main elements, symmetry, variety (μεταβολή), and departure from normal idiom (ἐξαλλαγή), and in treating the second of these, he had no difficulty in showing how the historian repeatedly softens a too rigorous balance by any one of a number of means tending to variety, for instance, by varying the construction of parallel clauses or by using a synonym instead of repeating a word. He explained the practice by showing that μεταβολή (ποικιλία) was regarded in antiquity as essential to an artistic style. Now Aristotle similarly emphasizes the importance of unusual and poetic words,[149] and, if the argument of the two preceding pages has any merit, then antithesis, associated as it was with the style of gnomic generalization, also sub-served the effect of dignity. In other words, to say that Thucydides sought symmetry and variety of expression and boldness of idiom is merely to say that, for the most part,

[148] For reference, see n. 8.
[149] *Rhet.* III 7.11. Unusual diction played an even greater part in fifth-century prose (*Rhet.* III 1.8–10, 2.5).

he followed the contemporary standards of artistic prose. Hence it is somewhat surprising when at the end of his monograph[150] Dr. Ros speaks of Thucydides' style as unique, and, though that judgment was based on his study of variety, still it naturally leads back to the main subject of this essay. For, as Dr. Ros observes, the principle of variety is merely, as it were, the obverse of the principle of symmetry, its purpose being to add subtlety and richness to an otherwise uniformly balanced style. It is therefore to be expected that the two practices would be found side by side and that when the one became widespread, so would the other.

In fact, as I tried to show in reviewing Dr. Ros's book,[151] the variety which he observes in the *History* is equally marked in Antiphon's Περὶ Ὁμονοίας. There is no need of repeating the evidence here; it is enough to say that Antiphon too alters his constructions, uses synonyms, and varies tense, mood, and number very much in the manner of the historian. Similarly, a list of such variations compiled from the *Medea* was sufficient to show that μεταβολή played its part beside antithesis and balance in the later tragic style which, it has been argued, was much influenced by the writings of the early sophists. Moreover, Antiphon's diction, like that of the sophists, included both the poetic and Ionic forms of tragedy and the newer but equally striking terminology of science. Hence it seems beyond question that, broadly speaking, Thucydides subscribed to the standards of artistic prose common during his early manhood, standards which, on the one hand, aimed at the dignity of new and searching generalizations and, on the other, embraced the unusual and varied diction of verse and

[150] Pages 458–63.
[151] *AJP* 61 (1940) 96–102.

science in a way quite foreign to the purer but more limited prose of the fourth century.

Yet, as Hermogenes remarked,[152] Thucydides' abstractness has something in common with the style of the Ἀλήθεια, which, however, as a technical work, quite lacks richness and variety but directs its balanced clauses almost wholly to the reason alone. Now in discussing Dr. Ros's book, I ventured to suggest that Thucydides did not seek variety for itself but had it, as it were, thrust upon him by what he conceived to be the nature of his task, namely, to observe the most rigorous and detailed accuracy and, at the same time, to set forth the broader aspects and underlying laws of political behavior. In other words, his *History* seeks to ally the specific and the general in a way not attempted in the purely abstract Ἀλήθεια, and thus it is cast in a style far more complex and subtle than the latter's, though, on the other hand, its underlying purpose has unquestionably something of the scientific ὑπόμνημα. Thus one could say that Thucydides employs the freer usages of artistic prose, as exemplified in the Περὶ Ὁμονοίας, for an end which resembles, though it far transcends, that of the Ἀλήθεια. And insofar as his purpose seems to have been unique, one could perhaps say that his style (being far more varied than that of the usual ὑπόμνημα or, conversely, more abstract than that of the epideixis) is likewise unique. Yet in making such a statement, one must remember that the elements of Thucydides' style—its symmetry, its variety, its boldness of diction—were fully consonant with the sophistic prose which he knew in Athens before his exile, and that his individuality consists merely in his use of these elements, in his blending, as it were, the styles of the ὑπόμνημα and the epideixis.

[152] See above, pp. 91–92.

Moreover, in regard to the speeches, one must remember that, with the exception of the fragment of Thrasymachus composed a dozen years after Thucydides left Athens, we have no example of a symbouleutic speech of the period covered by the *History*. One must, therefore, be very slow to assert that the Athenians at least among his speakers could not possibly have spoken in some such way as he says they did, especially when, apart from the general likelihood that a man brought up in Athens would instinctively adopt the manner in use there, we have the following reasons for believing in his essential accuracy. First, Thucydides undoubtedly conceived many of his own ideas in Athens; hence the likelihood exists that he likewise conceived there the general concept of his speeches. Then, many of the ideas and forms of argument actually used in the speeches are attested of the period when they were allegedly delivered, a fact which strengthens the previous assumption. Again, the antithetical style, relieved by variety and adorned by poetic and scientific words, was in all probability the creation, not of Gorgias whose mannerisms differ considerably from those of Thucydides, but of earlier sophists whose stylistic teachings are seen both in the prose of the sophist Antiphon and in the earliest extant plays of Sophocles and Euripides. Hence it seems unlikely that the Athenian public, accustomed to the antithetical debates of tragedy, would have expected to hear, or that Pericles, the friend of sophists, would have expected to deliver, a speech, the simple structure of which was merely decked by poeticisms and images.

Then, the practice not merely of Thucydides but of the tragedians (and, one could add, pseudo-Xenophon, although his work is seemingly an ὑπόμνημα written in a style even simpler than that of the ᾿Αλήθεια)[153] suggests that the

153 See above, n. 139.

Athenians of the fifth century, like other peoples in times of swiftly broadening horizons, preferred those general and inclusive ideas and forms of argument of the sort to which, it has been argued, antithesis was most appropriate both for reasons of clarity and because it was traditionally associated with the style of gnomic generalization. Stylistically such speeches must have combined the scientific abstractness of the ὑπόμνημα with the richness of the epideixis in some such way as Thucydides suggests. The point is important; for the generalizations of Thucydides' speeches have probably caused more people to doubt their accuracy than any other single element. And yet it is doubtful whether, once prose has become the subject of serious study, it can be expected to be simple and specific in an age of otherwise grandiose art. Certainly, the style of Addison could not have attended the verse of Shakespeare, but a great period of poetry seems naturally to issue in such poetic and complex prose as that of Thucydides' speeches or Milton's pamphlets.[154] Finally, as I suggested in my earlier essay,[155] the essential uniformity of style in the speeches (Thucydides characterizes his speakers largely by the ideas which they express rather than by their style) must in part at least reflect the actual practice of a period before marked individuality of speech developed. Only later did Lysias begin the fashion of matching speech to character; before then, a severe and formal type of oratory was doubtless fairly uniform precisely because not even Thrasymachus, with his simpler and more natural diction, wholly evolved a plain style to conflict with the more grandiose.

There is no doubt that Thucydides' speeches are more compressed and thus more abstruse than actual speeches

---

[154] Cf. W. R. M. Lamb, *Clio Enthroned* (Cambridge 1914) 308–12.
[155] Above, chap. I pp. 4–6, 52–53.

would have been. It is equally certain that they look to one another and play a vital part in his actual *History*. They may in addition be marked to some extent by the individuality which, as was suggested above, inhered in the very nature of the work. But, on the other hand, there is little reason to believe that the style even of the first speeches would have been inconceivable in the time when they purport to have been delivered. On the contrary; even these speeches are probably representative of the style which Thucydides heard about him and himself learned during his early manhood and many years later attempted to recapture in his *History*.

CHAPTER III

THE UNITY OF
THUCYDIDES' HISTORY

❧❧❧

I

The revival of the old controversy on when Thucydides composed the various parts of his *History*, although designed to prove the existence of many early parts in the work which we have, apparently tended to prove the opposite. The reason is that each new participant in the controversy, while advancing his own views, undermined those of his predecessor and hence diminished, rather than increased, the number of passages still capable of being regarded as early, with the result that it finally became possible to attack the whole position that the *History* contains many such passages. This evolution was, in brief, as follows. In 1919 Ed. Schwartz[1] seemingly opened a new era in the study of Thucydides when he urged that, of the four speeches at the council of Sparta reported in the first book, those of the Corinthians and of Archidamus were composed after the Peace of Nicias, while those of the Athenians and of the ephor Sthenelaidas were added after 404—an important observation, if true, since it would suggest that Thucydides once regarded Corinth as the cause of the war and only later saw Sparta's fear of Athens as the ἀληθεστάτη πρόφασις. A corollary was that, when in 404 Thucydides

[1] *Das Geschichtswerk des Thukydides*, Bonn 1919[1], 1929[2].

came to this new understanding of Sparta, he saw how right Pericles had been and accordingly completed his work with the purpose of vindicating the great statesman, who at that time was thought to have ruined Athens. The novelty of Schwartz's method, it will be seen, was to have identified early and late passages with the purpose of proving a development in Thucydides' thought. In the same year and the following, the method was carried further by Max Pohlenz,[2] who, however, disagreed with Schwartz's conclusions. After showing that the debate at Sparta in the first book is in fact a unit and thus late, he based his own view of Thucydides' development rather on his reading of the famous sentence in I 22.1, which he took as a promise by Thucydides to report speeches exactly. Since, however, many speeches can hardly be so described, Pohlenz went on to distinguish early from late speeches by the criterion of exactitude, discovering a development not so much in Thucydides' view of the war as in his methods of historiography. And nine years later[3] W. Schadewaldt pressed the same conclusion still further. Accepting Pohlenz' literalistic reading of I 22.1 and finding the same ideal of accuracy embodied in the Archaeology, he went on to contrast the methods seemingly adopted there with what he considered the far broader and more penetrating attitude revealed in books six and seven, both of which he argued were composed after 404. His deduction was striking: namely, that during the war Thucydides developed from an *historisierender Sophist*[4] interested only in the most literal accuracy to an historian in the fullest sense of the word, a man able to analyze the fundamental processes of state and society.

[2] "Thukydidesstudien," *Nachrichten von der kgl. Gesellschaft der Wissenschaften zu Göttingen* (1919) 95–138. (1920) 56–82.
[3] *Die Geschichtschreibung des Thukydides*, Berlin 1929.   [4] *Ibid.*, p. 30.

But it will be observed that in the course of this argument more and more parts of the *History* were continually being vindicated as late. The list now included books six and seven, those parts of books one which concern the rivalry of Athens and Sparta, and all passages contrasting Pericles' policies with those of his successors, a very broad topic indeed which would inevitably include all Pericles' speeches (except possibly some of the first), the estimate of him in II 65, the Mytilenean Debate, the analysis of στάσις, and such parts of the fourth book as are concerned with Athens' expansionist policies. Moreover, such passages as were still called early were so described on the reading of I 22.1 which made Thucydides seem to say that exactitude and only exactitude was the foundation of the *History*. But precisely this point was challenged in 1936 and 1937 by two young scholars, A. Grosskinsky[5] and H. Patzer,[6] whose successive studies showed beyond much doubt that Thucydides was not asserting mere accuracy as the basis of his speeches but that on the contrary, by his own words, the speeches were to contain primarily what he regarded as τὰ δέοντα, that is, the broad considerations justifying any given stand. Only secondarily were they to be limited by the ξύμπασα γνώμη of what was actually said—γνώμη meaning, in Patzer's able analysis, the essential relationship of a mind to a practical problem and thus signifying not so much the drift of one speech as the whole cast of a man's policy as revealed perhaps in several speeches. This interpretation of the first sentence in I 22 was confirmed, so these scholars maintained, by the famous last sentence: that is, the general considerations of a social and political sort

[5] "Das Programm des Thukydides," *Neue deutsche Forschungen*, Abt. klass. Phil., 1936.
[6] "Das Problem der Geschichtsschreibung des Thukydides und die Thukydideische Frage," *ibid.*, 1937.

contained in the speeches (τὰ δέοντα) were to be at least a chief means of expounding the recurrent tendencies of human nature (τὸ ἀνθρώπινον), on which Thucydides squarely rested the later value of his work. But with this broader and undoubtedly more correct interpretation of I 22, the whole theory by which Pohlenz and Schadewaldt had distinguished between early and late passages fell to the ground, and when a still later study, that of F. Bizer,[7] concluded that a late date fits the Archaeology far better than an early one, virtually nothing remained of the whole movement which had sought to find in the extant *History* strong traces of its author's development.

That is not to say that early passages may not exist in the *History*; it is inconceivable that Thucydides did not take notes or that he failed to use them when he wrote his final work. It is merely to say that the work which we have should not be regarded as an agglomeration of passages written at widely different times and imperfectly blended together by reason of the author's premature death, but rather as composed primarily at one time with the help of earlier notes and, if broken at the end and incomplete perhaps in several places, yet possessing after all the unity which might be expected to result from a period of more or less sustained composition. But if that or anything like that is the case, then the work should reveal a set of consistent ideas, organically developed from one end of the *History* to the other. Certainly, when Thucydides in the famous sentence just referred to speaks of the recurrency of historical events, he implies that the war followed some pattern and that he, as an historian, has expounded that pattern; otherwise it is hard to see what he could have imagined would be recurrent. Thus if one is to maintain that the

---

[7] *Untersuchungen zur Archäologie des Thukydides*, Tübingen diss. 1937.

History is in a fairly finished state as we have it and was composed essentially in one period of the author's life, it is not enough merely to prove how few passages imply an earlier version, valuable as that negative task is. It is necessary to show that the version which we have is in fact so complete a unit, that no part stands outside the complex of ideas known from other parts and that, since much of it is demonstrably late, all of it must accordingly have been composed or arranged at the same time—in sum, that it is the kind of work which a brilliant mind, dominated by a certain number of related ideas, would compose when those ideas were consistently before it. But it was natural that Grosskinsky and Patzer, faced as they were with the divisionistic arguments of their predecessors, should not have attempted this more positive task, and to find anything of the sort, it is necessary to return to Ed. Meyer's brilliant essay published in 1899.[8] To undertake once more so thorough an analysis as his is impossible here, but in view of the complicated nature of the controversy since he wrote, it may not be purposeless to explore again the grounds for believing in the unity of the *History*.

II

Perhaps the easiest way to do so will be to examine the leading ideas of books six and seven and then to trace these same ideas through the preceding books. For clearly, if Thucydides began composing his *History* after the end of the war or towards its close, he wrote even the first books with later events in mind, and the Sicilian narrative will consequently owe its climactic character to the fact that it draws together many strands of thought expounded previously. Now the opening books contain many passages

[8] *Forschungen zur alten Geschichte* (Halle 1899) II 269–436.

either certainly or probably written after 404,[9] and if one assumed that Thucydides began with the first sentence and wrote progressively to the last, then books six and seven would obviously fall towards the end of his period of authorship. There seems reason to believe that on the whole he did write consecutively. Thus in talking of Delos in V 1, he refers back to the purification described in III 104 with the words ᾗ πρότερόν μοι δεδήλωται;[10] in VI 94.1 he refers back to VI 4 in the same way; in VI 31.2 he compares the expeditionary army of 415 to the forces commanded successively by Pericles and Hagnon in 430, which are carefully described in II 56 and 58;[11] in introducing the account of the tyrannicides in VI 54.1, he uses the words ἐπὶ πλέον διηγησάμενος, which may, though they need not absolutely, mean that he is conscious of having treated the subject more briefly before in I 20; and in III 90.1 he says that he will note only the main points of the first Sicilian expedition, as if aware that it was of importance chiefly as foreshadowing the second. But even if these statements were more conclusive than they are, the probability would still remain that he would at times turn back to change or insert some passage. Thus it will not be maintained here that he wrote absolutely consecutively or that a given passage may not have been written after one that follows it (we cannot hope to follow such a delicate thing as composition with anything like complete accuracy), but only, as before said, that books six and seven are so closely knit with what precedes, that the whole work betrays a plan consistently worked out and therefore (it is natural to

[9] These passages are listed by Patzer, "Problem," pp. 103–7.

[10] Similarly VIII 108.4 refers to the moving of the Delians to Atramyttium described in V 1.

[11] In the same way VIII 15.1 mentions the restrictions on the reserve of 1000 talents noted in II 24.1.

suppose) worked out in a period of more or less sustained authorship.

But if so, the Sicilian narrative should not have been composed at a time too far removed from the late passages in the opening books referred to above—in other words, it should not have been composed directly after the expedition itself but near or after the end of the war—and there are in fact good grounds for assuming that to be the case. The most thorough discussion of the subject is Schadewaldt's,[12] who emphasized two passages especially: VII 57.2 where, in describing the forces at Syracuse, Thucydides lists as Athenian by origin καὶ Αἰγινῆται οἳ τότε Αἴγιναν εἶχον, presumably to distinguish them from the true Aeginetans restored to their native island in 405;[13] and VI 15.2–5, where, after noting Alcibiades' extravagance, he goes on ὅπερ καὶ καθεῖλεν ὕστερον τὴν τῶν Ἀθηναίων πόλιν οὐχ ἥκιστα and then explains that, through fear of his ambitions, the Athenians chose other generals and thus οὐ διὰ μακροῦ ἔσφηλαν τὴν πόλιν. The latter verb, limited by οὐ διὰ μακροῦ, Schadewaldt took as a reference to Athens' losses from the Sicilian expedition, but the former and stronger verb, less narrowly limited by ὕστερον, he interpreted as an allusion to her ultimate defeat.[14] Neither passage is perhaps entirely clinching (in the first, Thucydides might possibly be distinguishing the Athenians on Aegina from the exiles of 431 rather than from the repatriates of 405, and in the second, the verb καθεῖλεν might imply a period late in the war when Athens' weakness was apparent but her doom not yet complete). Yet the obvious and probable interpretation is certainly as made by Schadewaldt, and it is confirmed by several other passages implying a lapse of

[12] *Geschichtschreibung*, pp. 8–15.
[13] Xenophon, *Hell.* II 2.9.
[14] For further discussion of the passage, see below, nn. 21 and 28.

time between the actual expedition and Thucydides' account.

The first of these is the well-known comment on Andocides' testimony in regard to the mutilators of the Hermae (VI 60.2), in which, after stating the motives behind the testimony, he concludes, τὸ δὲ σαφὲς οὐδεὶς οὔτε τότε οὔτε ὕστερον ἔχει εἰπεῖν περὶ τῶν δρασάντων τὸ ἔργον. Without going into the many discrepancies in our accounts of the affair, it may be said that Andocides himself in 410 admitted and in 399 denied complicity in it[15] (a point on which Thucydides himself was doubtful, as is clear from the next sentence to that just quoted), and that the remark in any case posits some inquiry on the latter's part, which in view of his exile would have been neither swift nor easy. Similar in its implications is the account of Decelea in VII 27 and 28, formally a digression to explain why Athens could not afford to keep the Thracian mercenaries which had arrived in the summer of 413 but actually a treatment of the whole effect of Decelea on the later course of the war. Thus the tone of the passage is forward-looking: in 27.3, the building of the fort by the assembled Peloponnesians is contrasted with its later occupation by successive garrisons; in 27.4, it is said that at times large contingents were there (Steup appositely cites VIII 71.1, where Agis in 411 is said to have summoned such a contingent) and at times only enough troops for raiding; in the same section Agis' continued residence there is emphasized, a passage which looks forward to VIII 5.3 and 70.2;[16] and in 28.1 the new difficulties of trade with Euboea are mentioned, another passage which looks forward to the later narrative in VIII 4 and 96.2. These references are not exact, but they undoubtedly

---

[15] *De Red.* 7 and 25, *De Myst.* 61–64. Jebb, *Attic Orators*, I, pp. 76–79.
[16] That Agis stayed largely at Decelea until the end of the war is clear from Xen. *Hell.* I 1.33, II 2.7, 3.3.

assume a knowledge of events for some years after 413 and quite possibly to the end of the war. The same deduction must be drawn from a number of superlatives in the sixth and seventh books. These are: first, the statement that the disaster at Mycalessus was ξυμφορὰ τῇ πόλει πάσῃ οὐδεμιᾶς ἥσσων μᾶλλον ἑτέρας (VII 29.5); then the remark on the νυκτομαχία on Epipolae, μόνη δὴ στρατοπέδων μεγάλων ἔν γε τῷδε τῷ πολέμῳ ἐγένετο (VII 44.1); again, the judgment preceding the catalogue of peoples engaged in the great final battle, ἔθνη πλεῖστα δὴ ἐπὶ μίαν πόλιν ταύτην ξυνῆλθε, πλήν γε δὴ τοῦ ξύμπαντος λόγου τοῦ ἐν τῷδε τῷ πολέμῳ πρὸς τὴν Ἀθηναίων τε πόλιν καὶ Λακεδαιμονίων (VII 56.4); further, the general assertion on the Athenian defeat at Syracuse, μέγιστον δὴ τὸ διάφορον τοῦτο [τῷ] Ἑλληνικῷ στρατεύματι ἐγένετο (VII 75.7); and finally, the crowning judgment on the expedition, ξυνέβη τε ἔργον τοῦτο [Ἑλληνικὸν] τῶν κατὰ τὸν πόλεμον τόνδε μέγιστον γενέσθαι, δοκεῖν δ' ἔμοιγε καὶ ὧν ἀκοῇ Ἑλληνικῶν ἴσμεν (VII 87.5). To say that Thucydides made these statements in ignorance of what might presently take place is to liken him to the poets and logographers whose uncritical stories he attacks in I 21; it is also to neglect several other passages where he carefully guards against extreme statement when he believes his knowledge inadequate (III 113.6; V 68.2, 74.3; VII 87.4). But indeed in the second, third, and last of the passages just quoted, he is evidently referring to the whole war, and there seems no good reason not to take him at his word.

Thus a number of statements in the Sicilian narrative were in all probability composed after the end of the war, and that these passages were not inserted into an earlier draft seems to follow from the generally recognized fact that books six and seven, more than any other part of the *History*, comprise a unified and consistent whole. Schadewaldt, who has also discussed this aspect of the Sicilian narrative,[17] has shown how difficult it in fact is to detach any of its important parts from their present context, and there is perhaps no need of restating his arguments here. The advocates of an early date, on the other hand, have had to rely chiefly on Thucydides' seeming ignorance of the future in such passages as VI 62.2 and VII 58.2, where he writes in the present tense of Himera, although it was destroyed by the Carthaginians in 409[18]—an argument almost entirely invalidated since Patzer has shown that Thucydides elsewhere uses such historical presents even of towns the destruction of which he himself notes.[19] It is certainly his habit (itself the result of his intensity of mind) to confine himself rather strictly to what he is describing at the moment; he glances at the future for the most part only when ideas that interest him greatly are involved, as, for instance, in his estimate of Pericles in II 65 or his remarks quoted above on the magnitude of the Sicilian expedition.[20] It would therefore be unreasonable, even without Patzer's observations, to expect him always to treat the later history of what he mentions merely in passing. An argument of another sort is that of A. Rehm,[21] who found proof of incompleteness in what he argues were blanks in VII 4.1,

[17] *Geschichtschreibung*, esp. pp. 10–11. For further discussion see below pp. 132-33 and Patzer, "Problem," p. 31 n. 67.

[18] Xen. *Hell.* I 1.37; Diodorus XIII 62. Cf. K. Ziegler, *Phil. Woch.* 50 (1930) 195.

[19] "Problem," p. 14, where he quotes I 56.2, Ποτειδεάτας, οἳ οἰκοῦσιν ἐπὶ τῷ ἰσθμῷ τῆς Παλλήνης, whence they were driven in 430/29 (II 70). Similar is II 23.3, ἣν νέμονται Ὠρώπιοι Ἀθηναίων ὑπήκοοι, which accordingly need not have been written before 412/11 when the Boeotians took Oropos (VIII 60.1).

[20] See below, pp. 165–69.

[21] *Philologus* 89 (1934) 133–60. His further attempt to explain all late references in VI and VII as additions is unconvincing (cf. Patzer, above, n. 17). For instance, to delete the clause in VI 15.3 on the ruinous effects of Alcibiades' extravagance would involve deleting not only the rest of 15 but the opening of Alcibiades' speech (16), which is intended to illustrate the previous judgment. These passages, however, serve the vital purpose of acquainting the reader with the people's fears of Alcibiades which flared out during the incident of the Hermae (see also below, n. 28). Similarly, to delete the superlatives in VI and VII would be to destroy the whole architecture of these books (see below, pp. 132–33).

7.1, and 43.5 left to be filled in later with the name of a fort
temporarily forgotten by Thucydides. But acute as this
observation is, it proves only what would doubtless be
assumed in any case, that his untimely death robbed every
part of the *History*, even the most finished parts, of ultimate
revision. In sum, considering the number of late passages
in these books, the paucity and inconclusiveness of the
supposedly early passages, and above all the inherent difficulty in imagining that so tightly woven a narrative could
ever have been achieved by a process of insertion, it seems
fair to assume that books six and seven were written at a
time not far removed from the late passages already noted
in the preceding books. But if so, we may return to the
larger question set forth at the beginning of this section,
namely, what are the leading ideas of the Sicilian books
and how are these ideas connected with what has gone
before? For if this connection could be shown to be close,
then we could say that it represents, in effect, the pattern
which Thucydides detected in the events of his time and on
which he rested the future utility of his work. It would also
justify us in believing that the *History* is not, so to speak, a
notebook of passages composed at widely different times
but rather a unified interpretation of the war and, as such,
an interpretation possible only when his opinions were
matured and the facts before him. Finally, as has been said,
such a connection, if shown, would augment the valuable,
if inevitably negative, work of those who have disproved
many of the alleged indications of an earlier version, by
suggesting in a somewhat more positive way the threads of
unity in the version which we have.

Perhaps no ideas play a larger part in the Sicilian narrative
than the following four: the magnitude and decisiveness
of the struggle at Syracuse; the surprising nature (παράλογος)

of Athens' defeat; the fact that she was defeated by democratic Syracuse when oligarchic Sparta had proved an easy
adversary; and the reasons for the defeat inherent in the
character of her government and leadership. These ideas
will be discussed successively in their relation to the foregoing narrative.

(1) That the Athenian attack on Syracuse produced, to
Thucydides' mind, the greatest struggle in the 27-years war,
appears from several passages already quoted: VII 44.1 on
Epipolae as the largest night engagement; 56.4 on the final
battle in the harbor as involving the greatest number of
peoples (excepting the total number engaged in the whole
war); 75.7 on the Athenian retreat as signifying the supreme
reverse ever sustained by a Greek army; and 87.5 on the
whole struggle as the greatest ἔργον in the war and probably
in Greek history. In addition to these passages are: VI 31.1,
where the expeditionary force of 415 is called the most
expensive and the handsomest up to that time; 31.6, where
it is observed that the undertaking constituted the farthest
flight of Athenian ambition (μέγιστος ἤδη διάπλους ἀπὸ
τῆς οἰκείας καὶ ἐπὶ μεγίστῃ ἐλπίδι τῶν μελλόντων πρὸς
τὰ ὑπάρχοντα ἐπεχειρήθη); and VII 70.4, where the final
battle in the harbor is said to have brought together most
ships in the smallest space.[22] But since these statements
evidently embody two distinct ideas—first, that the expedition was on an extraordinarily large scale and second, that,
such being the case, its failure inflicted a supreme blow on
Athens—it may be well to consider the two ideas separately.

---

[22] To these should be added the contested passage, VII 85.4, on the slaughter
at the Assinarus: πλεῖστος γὰρ δὴ φόνος οὗτος καὶ οὐδενὸς ἐλάσσων τῶν ἐν
τῷ [Σικελικῷ] πολέμῳ τούτῳ ἐγένετο. The deletion of Σικελικῷ, recommended
by the scholiast, is supported by Marchant *ad loc.*, though opposed by Steup. The
apparent reference to Herodotus VII 170.3, the unusual addition of two modifiers
to πόλεμος, and the climactic tone of the preceding narrative seemingly argue for
deletion.

As for the first, there is an interesting passage in Alcibiades' first speech where he is made to say just before the expedition that the military efforts of all the Greek states had so far proved a good deal smaller than expected (οὔτε οἱ ἄλλοι Ἕλληνες διεφάνησαν τοσοῦτοι ὄντες ὅσους ἕκαστοι σφᾶς αὐτοὺς ἠρίθμουν, ἀλλὰ μέγιστον δὴ αὐτοὺς ἐψευσμένη ἡ Ἑλλὰς μόλις ἐν τῷδε τῷ πολέμῳ ἱκανῶς ὡπλίσθη, VI 17.5). Accepted by Hude and Marchant, the sentence was deleted by Classen on the insufficient grounds that so young a man could not have made such a statement, and by Steup because he thought that Alcibiades would not have spoken of a continuous state of war after the Peace of Nicias and before the formal revival of hostilities between Athens and Sparta in 413 (VII 18). But, as Patzer has shown in another connection,[23] a virtual state of war is assumed to exist at this time in several places, notably in the summary of the Egestians' speech (VI 6.2 *ad fin.*), in Nicias' first speech (VI 10.1), in Alcibiades' speech at Sparta (VI 91.6), and by Thucydides himself in VI 73.2, VII 28.3, and VI 105.1. If then the passage be accepted as genuine, we may assume that the historian and, presumably, Alcibiades as well regarded the war as only gradually gathering momentum. One reason for that view, so far at least as Athens is concerned, is several times expressed; it was, of course, the plague. Thus Nicias in warning against the expedition speaks of the city as even then only partially recovered (VI 12.1), and Thucydides later says the same, though without Nicias' reservations (26.2). Now, as has been pointed out already, when he comes to discuss the unparalleled scale of the original expeditionary force (VI 31.2), he compares it to that of 430 which is carefully described in the second book (56 and 58). His point is that the earlier venture, undertaken when the plague

[23] "Problem," pp. 19–20.

had just begun, represented Athens' finest combined force of ships and hoplites before 415. Similarly, in speaking of the invasion of Megara in 431 (which as a land attack could not later have been compared to the Sicilian expedition), he says, στρατόπεδόν τε μέγιστον δὴ τοῦτο ἀθρόον 'Αθηναίων ἐγένετο, ἀκμαζούσης ἔτι τῆς πόλεως καὶ οὔπω νενοσηκυίας (II 31.2). Again, in talking of the second epidemic of 426 (III 87.2), he says that nothing weakened Athens more than the plague.[24] Thus these passages give a consistent answer to the question why the Athenians did not produce their full strength at once and why therefore the Sicilian expedition was the climax of the war. An explanation is likewise given for Sparta's slow beginning. In the first place, as is repeatedly stressed, the Spartans were naturally torpid and conservative (I 70, 118.2, 132.5; IV 55.2; V 63.2; VI 88.10; VIII 96.5); then, with the exception seemingly of a few individuals like Archidamus (I 80–81), they expected the time-honored strategy of invasion to win them a quick victory (I 121.4, IV 85.2, V 14.3, VII 28.3, VIII 24.5). Thus they were amazed that Athens did not desist even when the revolt of Mytilene was added to the ravaging of Attica (III 16.2), and after the defeat of Pylos they were completely shaken, feeling unable to cope with so unusual an adversary (IV 55). Hence when Brasidas, whose quite un-Spartan energy is often noted (cf. esp. IV 81.1), attacked the Thraceward country, it was felt that they were just beginning to fight (τὸ πρῶτον Λακεδαιμονίων ὀργώντων ἔμελλον πειράσεσθαι, IV 108.6). Both he, however, and his conquests

---

[24] It has been argued that this passage could not have been written after the Sicilian expedition (cf. Steup *ad loc.* but also Patzer, "Problem," p. 108). It is doubtful, however, whether the remark should be interpreted so strictly. It merely reinforces what has been said of the plague in II 54.1 and in Pericles' last speech (II 64.1–3, where there is a similar juxtaposition of the idea of Athens' δύναμις). Absorbed in the period which he is describing (see below, pp. 166–69), Thucydides seems to be making a statement quite true of that time without reference to disasters of another sort which took place later.

were neglected by the home government, which after the Peace of Nicias was accordingly criticized even more fiercely for its sloth and cowardice. Hence it was that the campaign of Mantinea seemed to Thucydides so significant a turning point: not only did it clear Sparta of the charge of μαλακία, ἀβουλία and βραδυτής (V 75.3; cf. I 122.4) but, what is more important in the present context, it actually called forth the finest Spartan army up to that time (στρατόπεδον δὴ τοῦτο κάλλιστον Ἑλληνικὸν τῶν μέχρι τοῦδε ξυνῆλθεν, V 60.3), with the result that the battle itself could be described as πλείστου δὴ χρόνου μεγίστη δὴ τῶν Ἑλληνικῶν καὶ ὑπὸ ἀξιολογωτάτων πόλεων ξυνελθοῦσα (V 74.1). Thus what is said before the sixth book not only of Athens' but of Sparta's military efforts bears out the statement of Alcibiades quoted above and, by so doing, prepares the gound for the climactic descriptions of the whole Sicilian narrative.

Here then we have followed one part of that recurrent and interwoven complex of ideas around which the *History* is built, and that Thucydides' analysis of the Spartans[25] came up in this connection (an analysis which in its entire consistency stands as one more proof that the work was conceived as a unit) suggests how a given idea is constantly invoking another, in such a way that, as the *History* advances, it draws increasingly on all that has gone before. But to confine ourselves still to the idea of magnitude, it is to be observed that these statements regarding the size of the war are not mere notes appended to the descriptions of certain

[25] Spartan traits, other than those noted above, are: their harshness as governors, I 77.6, 95.1, 103.1, III 93.2, V 52.1, VIII 84 (but contrast Brasidas, IV 81.2); their fear of the helots, I 132.4, IV 41.3, 55.1, V 14.3, VII 26.2, VIII 40.2; their religiosity, II 72.2, III 89.1, V 54.2, 55.3, VII 18; their secrecy, I 92.1, II 39.1, V 68.2; their suspiciousness, I 68.2, 90.2, 102.3, III 13, V 109; their justice towards one another, I 132.5, V 105.4; their covert pursuance of their own ξυμφέρον, I 76.2, 102.3, III 68.4, V 105.4; their discipline, I 84, II 11, IV 40, V 9, 72.3.

events but constitute, as it were, fixed landmarks in the total structure. Thus, when in VI 31 Thucydides describes the supreme size, brilliance, and efficiency of the first Athenian flotilla and then, after retailing the later reinforcements and noting with various superlatives the growing fierceness of the struggle, rises at last to the great catalogue of peoples engaged in the final battle (VII 57–58), he is clearly preparing for the ultimate catastrophe, a catastrophe which is itself marked by the assertions that Athens' loss was the worst ever sustained by a Greek city and that the whole ἔργον was unmatched either in the war or, to his own mind, in all Greek experience (VII 87). No better proof is to be found that books six and seven were conceived as a unit than in these progressive, interrelated statements, but, what is more important, their significance cannot be limited to the Sicilian books alone. For when it is said in the first and second sentences of the *History* that the war about to be described was the greatest of all Greek wars and, in the sixth and seventh books, that it reached its climax in the struggle at Syracuse, the relation of these separate statements can hardly be accidental. One therefore concludes on these grounds alone (quite apart from the other indications of the Archaeology's late date),[26] that he wrote each part with the other in mind, and consequently that an orderly and consistent progression exists from the initial claim regarding the size of the war, through the various explanations why Athens and Sparta got rather slowly under way, to the full corroboration of the first claim in the Sicilian books.

With so much on the mere magnitude of the war in Sicily, we may turn to the corollary of the idea noted above, namely, the decisiveness of the struggle in the total 27-years war. Four passages already quoted perhaps best express the

[26] See below, pp. 140–42, 160, 167–68.

seriousness of Athens' loss:[27] VI 15.3, where it is said that Alcibiades' extravagance καθεῖλεν ὕστερον τὴν ... πόλιν; VII 28, on Athens' impoverishment under the double burden of the Sicilian war and the Spartan occupation of Decelea; VII 75.2, the famous description of the retreat from Syracuse, beginning δεινὸν οὖν ἦν ... ὅτι τάς τε ναῦς ἀπολωλεκότες πάσας ἀπεχώρουν καὶ ἀντὶ μεγάλης ἐλπίδος καὶ αὐτοὶ καὶ ἡ πόλις κινδυνεύοντες; and VII 87.5, where after noting the magnitude of the ἔργον, Thucydides adds that it was τοῖς τε κρατήσασι λαμπρότατον καὶ τοῖς διαφθαρεῖσι δυστυχέστατον, continuing πανωλεθρίᾳ δὴ τὸ λεγόμενον καὶ πεζὸς καὶ νῆες καὶ οὐδὲν ὅτι οὐκ ἀπώλετο. It has been shown already that these statements could hardly have been written before the end of the war and, that being the case, they reveal quite clearly how important an element in Athens' ultimate defeat Thucydides considered the expedition. Thus it should be expected that the rest of the narrative, if conceived as a unit at the end of the war, should reveal this same idea, and although it is true, as observed above, that Thucydides does not commonly anticipate the future and therefore would not often refer to the expedition in the previous books, nevertheless many passages undoubtedly look to this great later event. The best known and oftenest referred to is the estimate of Pericles in II 65, where after contrasting the latter's wise leadership with that of his successors, Thucydides goes on to say that their greatest error was the Sicilian expedition, and then observes wonderingly that, even after it, the Athenians, although already in revolution, were able to hold out for several years against their original enemy, the latter's Sicilian reinforcements, their own revolting subjects, and Cyrus. Now it will be observed that this passage, while confirming

[27] See also in Nicias' speeches VII 64, 77.7.

the central importance of the Sicilian war, regards Athens' actual losses from it as only one of several factors in her ultimate defeat, the others being the blind self-interest of her politicians, the ensuing disunity of the city, and the consequent squandering of the great advantages on the basis of which Pericles had justly predicted victory. More will be said of these ideas below (pp. 154–62), but it should be noted here that, precisely by considering the expedition as the supreme evidence and result of Athens' internal faults, does Thucydides bind the whole *History* together as closely as he does. For so considered, it becomes inseparable from Pericles' warning against foreign conquests (I 144.1, II 65.7), from the Mytilenean Debate and the description of στάσις (which merely carry further what is said in II 65 of the Athenian politicians), from Cleon's refusal of peace after Pylos (which reveals the same desire for conquest that was warned against by Pericles but supremely exemplified at Syracuse), and from the Melian Dialogue. But further still, when he says in II 65 that the expedition failed for political reasons rather than because the plan was impossible, and then goes on to observe that the city, shattered though it was, could still hold out for several years, he invokes still another vital concept of the *History*, namely, that of Athens' extraordinary strength. It is this concept which forms the burden of the first book, where from the Archaeology on, Thucydides expounds the greatness of Athens' power—a power based, like that of Minos and Agamemnon, on control of the sea, therefore positing, like theirs, a great economic advance, and consequently invulnerable to an outmoded land state like Sparta (see below, pp. 140–42). We have already seen that the superlatives of the sixth and seventh books are inseparable from the initial statements on the magnitude of the war, but it must also be noted that

that magnitude itself depended on the high condition of the belligerent states, and notably that of Athens since she opposed all the others. But to the degree that the Sicilian expedition represented the highest pitch of Athens' strength, was its failure the more serious. When therefore Thucydides, while recognizing that fact, admiringly notes her ability to resist some years more, he is tying the catastrophic descriptions of the sixth and seventh books all the more tightly to the analysis of Athens' strength which had gone before. Hence II 65 sets the Sicilian expedition not only in the perspective of Athens' political weakness, of which more will be said presently, but also in that of her great initial strength which, as the burden of the first book, provides the basis of Pericles' confident prognosis (I 141.2–144).

A word should finally be added concerning the eighth book, since this concept of the magnitude and the decisiveness of the Sicilian expedition should be expected to reveal itself there as well. Now one of the reasons[28] advanced by

[28] H. Strasburger, *Philologus* 91 (1936) 137–52. He therefore concludes that the remark on Alcibiades' extravagance, ὅπερ καὶ καθεῖλεν ὕστερον τὴν ... πόλιν οὐχ ἥκιστα (VI 15.3), applies to the disaster of 413, not as Schadewaldt had argued, to that of 404 (see above, p. 124). His argument is (pp. 148–49) that Alcibiades here appears as the cause of Athens' ruin, whereas in II 65 the cause is said to have lain in the nature of Athenian democracy. There can be no doubt that the latter view represents Thucydides' deeper judgment. On the other hand, it is by no means neglected in VI and VII (which accordingly were not written from a different point of view from that expressed in II 65, see below, pp. 154–62), nor is it incompatible with the above statement in regard to Alcibiades, for two reasons. First, one of the grounds given in II 65 for Pericles' ascendancy is that he was χρημάτων διαφανῶς ἀδωρότατος (II 65.8, cf. II 13.1, where he is said to have relinquished his estates voluntarily, and below, pp. 157–58). Hence, unlike Alcibiades, he gave his opponents no handle against him. When therefore Thucydides in VI 15 stresses the latter's enormous extravagance, he is reverting to his train of thought in II 65, though with a difference of emphasis caused by the impression of Alcibiades' dissolute life. Second, it is unreasonable to claim that the words ὅπερ καθεῖλεν ὕστερον τὴν πόλιν οὐχ ἥκιστα exclude the other and deeper cause of Athens' defeat noted in II 65, since to do so is to say that Thucydides was interested only in theoretical problems. He was, however, equally interested in the effect of specific events, and the superlatives noted above show that even after 404 he continued to regard the Sicilian venture as a staggering blow to Athens. Hence when he says that Alcibiades' extravagance was "not the least" cause of Athens' ruin (οὐχ ἥκιστα, i.e. one of several causes), he is saying virtually what he says in those superlatives. His mind is on the losses which might have been avoided if

those who have argued that books six and seven were written soon after the event is that the great emphasis there placed on Athens' defeat seemed incompatible with the offers of peace refused by her after Cyzicus in 410,[29] as again in 407 and 406. This view is of course untenable, if the foregoing arguments on the unity and lateness of the Sicilian books be accepted, but (even neglecting those arguments) it is also untenable if, as seems the case, the eighth book was written in close connection with books six and seven. It has already been observed (p. 125) that what is said in VII 28 of the strain on Athens resulting from the occupation of Decelea, of Agis' residence there, and of Athens' new dependence on sea traffic with Euboea, certainly looks to continuing passages in the eighth book. But many other parts of the latter conspicuously repeat ideas or turns of expression already familiar from what has just preceded: for instance, the remarks on the Athenian colonists on Aegina (VII 57.2, VIII 69.3); the repeated expressions ὀλίγον οὐδέν and ἀγώνισμα (VII 59.3, 87.6; VIII 15.2; VII 56.2, 59.2, 86.2; VIII 12.2, 17.2); Alcibiades' practice of justifying himself on the grounds of his ἰδία ξυμφορά (VI 92.2, VIII 81.2); the conception that soldiers in a democracy are freest in criticizing their officers (VII 14.2, VIII 84.2); the judgment that, in preventing the Athenians on Samos from attacking

---

Alcibiades had not been dismissed from office, and though he can elsewhere regard that dismissal as in turn lodged in the nature of democracy, still it was in itself a decisive turning point, as he says in II 65.11. Thus although the statement is less profound and less general than that of II 65, it is wholly consistent with it. It is moreover the natural statement at just this point in the narrative when Alcibiades is about to speak and the whole tragic sequence of events is about to unroll. For the immediate cause of what followed at Athens, Sparta, Decelea, and Syracuse was in fact this same self-interested extravagance, and to say that Thucydides could not have spoken of it in this way after 404 is to say that he did not then consider the following events important, which we know not to have been the case. Thus καθεῖλεν does glance, though unobtrusively, at the whole later fate of Athens, a fuller diagnosis of which is given in II 65.

[29] Diodorus XIII 53–54.

the home-city, Alcibiades for the first time acted out of genuine patriotism (VIII 86.4, a contrast to VI 15); the view that democracy at its best is a mixed government, not a domination by the poorer classes (VI 39, VIII 97.2, to which compare the distinction drawn by Alcibiades at Sparta, VI 89.6, between a government based on τὸ ξύμπαν and one representing the πονηροί). Many more such passages could be adduced, but the above perhaps sufficiently illustrate the close continuity between the Sicilian narrative and the eighth book. But the latter was certainly written after Cyzicus, since VIII 97.2 assumes a knowledge of the decline of the five thousand.[30] Consequently, the Sicilian books as well as the eighth book must, on any view, have been composed after the offer of peace in 410, and it cannot therefore be asserted that, in emphasizing the greatness of Athens' loss in Sicily, Thucydides failed to reckon with her partial later recovery. But the fact is that he himself explains this seeming contradiction not only satisfactorily but in a manner quite consistent with his whole narrative. His explanation falls into three parts: first, that though the Athenians were fearfully shaken after Syracuse, they once again demonstrated their great inherent strength (and once again, to their enemy's great surprise), by mustering the ability to continue (II 65.12; IV 108.4; VIII 2.1-2, 24.5, 106.5); second, that they were enabled gradually to regain confidence because the Spartans, in spite of Agis' greater vigor, once again showed themselves unable to press home an advantage and thus remained as before the easiest possible antagonists for Athens (VIII 96.4-5); and finally, that, so far at least as the period covered

[30] For the effect of Cyzicus in restoring democracy at Athens, see F. E. Adcock in *CAH* V 343-46, and W. S. Ferguson, *ibid.*, 485. VIII 47.1, where Alcibiades is said to have foreseen ὅτι ἔσται ποτὲ αὐτῷ πείσαντι κατελθεῖν, may well envisage his actual return to Athens in 407, rather than the mere rescinding of his banishment noted in VIII 97.3.

by the eighth book is concerned, the Athenians were able to transcend those revolutionary movements which, as was observed in II 65, in the long run joined with the evil consequences of Syracuse to prove their ruin (VIII 1.3-4, 97.2). Enough has been said on the connection of these first two concepts (those, namely, of Athens' great inherent strength and of the slowness of Sparta) with the preceding narrative, but it may perhaps be observed of the third, that the Sicilian venture had, to Thucydides' mind, a certain revolutionary character. At least, as will be shown more fully below (pp. 154-62), he makes quite clear that the demos favored the expedition in the hope of more lucrative employment in an extended empire, and hence that the expedition represented the expansionist policies of the extreme democrats as much as did Cleon's refusal of peace or his abortive Boeotian campaign. Thus when in the very opening section of the eighth book Thucydides observes the new reasonability and temperance of the demos and later goes on to praise the restraining constitution proposed in 411 (VIII 97.2), he is following a line of thought which extends clear through the *History*, beginning with Pericles' plea for a moderate (that is, a nonexpansionist) policy and a united people. Had he lived to describe Cleophon's refusal of peace after Cyzicus, he would doubtless have seen in it merely one more example of that extremism which had not only underlain all Athens' great reverses but, as the war advanced, had produced a condition perhaps even more fatal to empire, namely, the reaction towards oligarchy (VIII 48.5-7). Thus, to conclude with this whole idea of the magnitude and seriousness of the Sicilian war, it is clear that Thucydides concurrently regards Athens' losses from two points of view: first, as shattering in themselves because of the mere size of the venture, and, second, as symbolizing and (by reason of the resultant poverty) to some extent producing that extremism and disunity which were Athens' supreme weakness. It is also clear that these ideas, and consequently the Sicilian books themselves, are planted firmly in the total structure of his work.

(2) A second concept which runs through the entire *History* and forms a strong band of unity within it is that conveyed by the word παράλογος. At first sight merely a term casually, if often, used by Thucydides, the word in fact conveys, perhaps more neatly than any other, one of his essential theses in regard to the war and therefore demands some attention. As has been observed already, Athens was expected to submit after a very few years of fighting (I 121.4, IV 85.2, V 14.3, VII 28.3, VIII 24.5); the belief, reiterated as it is throughout the *History*, shows with how much greater a military reputation Sparta entered the war. It has also been observed that Archidamus doubted his country's ability to win on the grounds that Athens' enormous economic and naval advance had at last made her invulnerable to the old-fashioned strategy of invasion. But, as Thucydides notes (I 87.3), he had few adherents, and the Spartans evidently plunged into war in the expectation that it would soon be over. It need hardly be said, however, that Archidamus' view fully coincided with that of Pericles, whose first and third speeches are devoted largely to showing why Athens had nothing to fear from a power which, though it ravaged Attica, could in no manner affect the basis of Athens' strength in her revenues, her access to materials, and her navy. But what most concerns ourselves is that Thucydides also both shared and deeply reflected on that view, so much so in fact that in the Archaeology he projects it into the remote past and finds there the same pattern of change that he believed exempli-

fied in the world about him. His argument is that Minos and Agamemnon, by establishing centralized authority and thus transcending the previously existent state of localism, gave rise to a stage of material civilization unlike anything that had gone before, and that the means by which they achieved this advance was naval power (cf. esp. I 8.3, 15.1). After their fall, he continues (I 13), the process might have been repeated by the naval states of Corinth and Samos had it not been checked, in the one case, by the timorous policy of the tyrants (I 17) and, in the other, by the advance of the Persians (I 16). When, therefore, he goes on later in the first book to praise Themistocles' genius in foreseeing the future significance of Athens' navy and in taking all practical steps to enlarge it (I 93.3–4, 138.3), he is evidently harking back to the thesis of the Archaeology, that centralism means both power and progress and that, in Greek history, the highroad to such power had always been command of the seas. For land states, as he specifically notes, had never been great (I 15.2). The conclusion therefore follows that Sparta, to his mind, had been strong, as it were, for the negative reason that no naval powers had come into existence in the period between the fall of Mycenae and the rise of Athens, although, as will be observed later (p. 160), the stability of her constitution, also noted in the Archaeology (I 18.1), was a factor in her strength. Accordingly, when Pericles maintained and even extended the naval policies of Themistocles,[31] he was, so to speak, reapplying the ancient secret of power which Minos and Agamemnon had used before him. Indeed, one could almost say that, to Thucydides' eyes, he was creating a state as much stronger and more progressive than such outmoded

[31] Compare the similar judgments on Attic policy attributed to the two men in I 91.4 and 140.5.

Three Essays on Thucydides

land states as Sparta as were the realms of Minos and Agamemnon than the communities before them. But, as has been said, not all persons realized this fact, and because Sparta had been strong, it was expected that she would continue so. Here then is the underlying meaning of the word παράλογος: it signifies the shock and surprise felt by all who (unlike Pericles and the historian himself) were unable to estimate the true sources of power and thus failed to see that the naval empire of Athens, eliciting as it had a great era of economic and technical advance, had virtually ushered in a new age of Greek history.

By this argument, then, the Archaeology stands closely woven in the texture of the *History* not only because it explains the magnitude of the war but also because it presents historical (one could almost say formal) analogies to the growth of Attic power, a power which was to visit many painful shocks upon the enemy and was to be destroyed not so much by them as by the Athenians themselves. But before we pursue this idea of surprise throughout the *History*, it may be well to note very briefly those qualities of mind which the acquisition of power, especially of naval power, had bred in the Athenians. In the first place, their skill at sea, entailing as it did an exact training in many maneuvers, constituted an ἐπιστήμη,[32] which in turn derived from an experience (ἐμπειρία[33]) continuous since the Persian wars. (It is to be observed from the references given here and below that these ideas are brought into play continually throughout the work and thus provide one more indication of its unity.) Then, their skill and, in a larger sense, their power derived from certain inward qualities:

[32] I 121.4, 142.6–9, II 89.8, III 78, VI 18.6, 68.2, 69.1, VII 36.4, 49.2, 62.2.
[33] I 18.3, 71.3, 99.3, 142.5, II 85.2, 89.3, IV 10.5, VI 18.6, 72.3, VII 21.3, 49.2, 61, 63.4.

high spirit (προθυμία[34]), courage (τόλμα, τολμηρόν[35]), capacity for innovation (νεωτεροποιία[36]), and willingness to undergo toils.[37] These qualities, noted in the famous contrast between the Athenians and the Spartans in I 70, as in several similar contrasts later (II 39, IV 55.2, VIII 96.5), explain the growing enmity between the two states described in the Pentecontaetia (cf. esp. I 102.3); they also convey what the allies of Athens forfeited on substituting money for service as their contribution to the Delian League (I 99). But they are chiefly stressed perhaps in two other contexts: first, as justifying Athens' original rise to power when Sparta voluntarily retired from the war against Persia (I 74.1–2, 90.1, 91.5; II 36.4; VI 83.1), and second, as inspiring the democratic doctrine of πολυπραγμοσύνη, the doctrine that those who deserve power should have it.[38] No concept is perhaps more central to the process of change which Thucydides is describing, and whether it be considered by itself in the speeches of Pericles (II 63–64), Alcibiades (VI 18), and Euphemus (VI 87) or in contrast to the conservative doctrine of ἡσυχία which Archidamus expounds (I 84) and with adherence to which Nicias is taxed (VI 18.6), it connotes democracy as opposed to oligarchy, freedom as opposed to discipline, and change as opposed to maintenance of the status quo. And finally, since the above-mentioned qualities are thus connected in Thucydides' mind with the institution of democracy, it becomes of interest to note exactly how he envisages that connection. The subject will be taken up further in the next section, but it may be said here that naval power to any Greek postulated a numerous and a free demos. Hence it is that the

[34] I 74.1–2, II 64.6, VI 18.2, 31.3, 83.1, 98.
[35] I 70.3, 90.1, 102.3, II 39.4, 88.2, IV 55.2, VI 31.6, VII 21.3, 28.3.
[36] I 70.2, 102.3.
[37] I 70.6, II 63, 64.3, VI 87.3.
[38] For further discussion, see above, chap. I pp. 26–28.

Funeral Oration conceives of democracy as permitting free play to initiative and as thereby reaping the benefits of an enlarged commerce, an improved standard of living, and a general sense of self-trust on the part of the citizenry. Indeed, as will appear below (p. 150), Thucydides probably thought of democracy as a prerequisite of material progress, since he specifically notes that the Athenians never met their match until they encountered the Syracusans who were ὁμοιότροποι with themselves. It is of course equally true that democracy, to his mind, ran the risk of political follies, follies which in fact cost Athens the war, but that he considered it at the same time one vital key to Athens' greatness must appear from what has just been said. Here in fact is the great dilemma of the *History*: how a state as progressive, and therefore as democratic, as Athens can nevertheless enjoy sane leadership under the stress of war and the hot demands of the populace. But for the present the important thing to notice is that the idea of παράλογος, signifying as it does the revelation of Athens' enormous vigor and enterprise, cannot be dissociated from the concept of change which, adumbrated in the Archaeology, is fully expressed in the pervasive contrast between an outmoded, oligarchic Sparta and her imperialistic, progressive, democratic rival.

Thus, to pursue this concept throughout the *History*, it takes its rise, as has been said, from the double thesis that Sparta, traditionally the great power of Greece, was expected to win but that in reality Athens (granted sane leadership) was certain of victory. References to the former idea have been given above (p. 140); the truth concerning Athens, as Thucydides saw it, is expounded early in the *History* in the Archaeology, parts of the Corinthians' and of Archidamus' speeches at Sparta, all Pericles' speeches, and the estimate of him in II 65. The first great surprise in the war (II 61.3), namely the plague, hardly concerns the present discussion except as it weakened Athens in the way described earlier. But the next time the word is used, namely, in the description of Phormio's naval victory of 429, it carries all the connotations sketched above, since the defeat of the far larger Peloponnesian fleet presented a signal (and to the Spartans a shocking) example of their enemy's daring, skill, and experience.[39] When again in the next year the Spartans were assured that Athens was crippled by the plague (III 13.3) and thus eagerly supported the revolting Mytileneans by a second invasion in the same season, to their great surprise the Athenians dispatched a hundred ships to the isthmus without moving the fleet already at Lesbos. They wished to show, Thucydides says, that the Spartans had quite mistaken their strength. The latter accordingly, ὁρῶντες πολὺν τὸν παράλογον, retired (III 16.2). The idea comes up several times in the fourth book, most notably in connection with the battle of Pylos, and its identical use here and in the seventh book provides perhaps one of the most striking proofs of unity in the whole work. There is, first, the paradox noted in 12.3 and 14.3, that in their opening assault on Demosthenes' position, the Spartans were attacking the Peloponnesus from the water, while the Athenians were defending it from the shore—a strange reversal of fortune, says Thucydides, since ἐν τῷ τότε the former were reputedly a land- and the latter a sea-power. The passage was therefore written, as has often been noted, sometime after the Athenian navy had broken down, presumably very late in the war or after it, and accordingly

[39] II 85.2, ἐδόκει γὰρ αὐτοῖς ἄλλως τε καὶ πρῶτον ναυμαχίας πειρασαμένοις πολὺς ὁ παράλογος εἶναι, καὶ οὐ τοσούτῳ ᾤοντο σφῶν τὸ ναυτικὸν λείπεσθαι, γεγενῆσθαι δέ τινα μαλακίαν, οὐκ ἀντιτιθέντες τὴν Ἀθηναίων ἐκ πολλοῦ ἐμπειρίαν τῆς σφετέρας δι' ὀλίγου μελέτης.

when he notes exactly the same paradox at the height of the Sicilian narrative—namely, that the Athenians retired from Syracuse πεζούς τε ἀντὶ ναυβατῶν πορευομένους καὶ ὁπλιτικῷ προσέχοντας μᾶλλον ἢ ναυτικῷ (VII 75.7)—the close connection between the two passages is inescapable. Similarly, the remark on the Athenians' plight before the final attack on Sphacteria, that they were μᾶλλον πολιορκούμενοι ἢ πολιορκοῦντες (IV 29.2), is virtually repeated in Nicias' letter (VII 11.4; cf. 75.7). But the final surrender of the Spartans provided of course the greatest surprise in this whole surprising series of events. Thucydides accordingly comments, παρὰ γνώμην τε δὴ μάλιστα τῶν κατὰ τὸν πόλεμον τοῦτο τοῖς Ἕλλησιν ἐγένετο (IV 40.1), a passage which harks back to the repeated previous assertions that, if the Spartans had nothing else, they had at least ἀνδρεία, and which also looks forward to the vindication of their courage at Mantinea (V 75.3). Finally, in reviewing the whole effect on Sparta both of this defeat and of that which followed at Cythera, Thucydides observes that the reverses, ἐν ὀλίγῳ ξυμβάντα παρὰ λόγον (IV 55.3), caused the Spartans supreme fright and adds that they now became extremely hesitant, the more so because they were fighting a naval war against the Athenians, οἷς τὸ μὴ ἐπιχειρούμενον αἰεὶ ἐλλιπὲς ἦν τῆς δοκήσεώς τι πράξειν. Almost an exact repetition of the Corinthians' remarks in I 70.7, the words resume the impression of both sides which has hitherto been built up. But it is to be observed that they also coincide with what is said of the shock to Athens after the defeat at Syracuse (κατάπληξις μεγίστη δή, VIII 1.2; ἔκπληξιν μεγίστην, IV 55.3) and to the judgment in VIII 96.5, that the Spartans remained to the last a most convenient adversary, a passage also closely similar to I 70. In sum, the narrative of Pylos is tightly bound both to what precedes

and to what follows, and its particularly close connection
with the Sicilian narrative (a connection reinforced, as will
appear presently, by what is said in both places of Athens'
expansionist policies) shows that Thucydides regarded the
two reverses as in many ways similar. Indeed he himself
compares them in VII 71.7. But what is to be observed
especially is that neither account could have been written
without an eye to the other; in fact neither account could
have been written without an eye to much of the *History*,
since the concept of παράλογος is both itself continuous
and depends on a continuing contrast between Athens and
Sparta.

But to go on, the idea comes up three times again in the
fourth book: in IV 65.4, where, after noting the punishment
of the generals who had made peace in Sicily, Thucydides
criticizes the ignorance and folly of the Athenians for
thinking that so great an island could have been subdued
by a small force and adds that their unexpected success had
made them too optimistic (a statement which looks back
to Cleon's confident refusal of peace in IV 21 and ahead to
an identical judgment on the Athenians' ignorance of Sicily
in VI 1); in IV 85.2, a passage already cited, where Brasidas
speaks of the Spartans as being deceived in their hopes of a
quick victory; and in IV 108.4 where Thucydides notes that
after the fall of Amphipolis many Thraceward towns
deserted Athens and goes on, καὶ γὰρ καὶ ἄδεια ἐφαίνετο
αὐτοῖς ἐψευσμένοις μὲν τῆς Ἀθηναίων δυνάμεως ἐπὶ
τοσοῦτον ὅση ὕστερον διεφάνη (a passage which confirms
all that has been said hitherto of Athens' strength and of the
Syracusan expedition as the climax of the war and which is
also echoed in VIII 2 and 24). In the fifth book (14.3) the
statement that the ten years' war had gone παρὰ γνώμην
for Sparta is repeated. But, as has been suggested, it is in the

Sicilian books that the idea achieves its greatest prominence, and when at the climax the Athenians are portrayed as themselves experiencing the sense of shocked surprise which they had formerly inflicted on others, one must conclude that the entire previous narrative has worked up to this reverse, and consequently that, in this respect also, the Sicilian books are an integral part of the whole. All the superlatives hitherto noted in regard to the scale of the expedition of course bear out the notion that it was a supreme (and to many a supremely surprising) revelation of Athens' strength. Thus Thucydides prefaces his description of the first flotilla by noting that the venture seemed an ἄπιστος διάνοια (VI 31.1), and Athenagoras is made to say in Syracuse that Athens could not conceivably attempt another war in addition to the one left unfinished in Greece (36.4). Indeed the historian himself repeats the idea with utmost emphasis in VII 28, when he says that no one would have believed that the Athenians, while themselves besieged, could be besieging others, καὶ τὸν παράλογον τοσοῦτον ποιῆσαι τοῖς Ἕλλησι τῆς δυνάμεως καὶ τόλμης, when at the beginning they had been expected not to survive two or three invasions. But even while he is making these statements, he is also stressing the unexpected character of the resistance at Syracuse (VI 34.6–8, VII 13.2), until with the great battle in the harbor the complete reverse takes place. Thus he can say before the battle, οἱ μὲν Ἀθηναῖοι ἐν παντὶ δὴ ἀθυμίας ἦσαν καὶ ὁ παράλογος αὐτοῖς μέγας ἦν (VII 55.1), and go on to observe that they had made no progress either by revolution or by arms, πόλεσι ταύταις μόναις ἤδη ὁμοιοτρόποις ἐπελθόντες, δημοκρατουμέναις τε, ὥσπερ καὶ αὐτοί, καὶ ναῦς καὶ ἵππους καὶ μεγέθη ἐχούσαις. The passage will come up again in the next section, but one must realize here that it is wholly consistent with what has gone before. For to say that the Athenians met their match only in democratic Syracuse is to revert to the whole concept of oligarchic Sparta as outmoded, of Athens as the stronger and more progressive power, and of Pericles' confident prediction that she would win if she avoided risks. When then the utter reverse pictured in VII 75 and resumed in the final chapter takes place, the reason for it is clear—the Athenians had committed errors which might have passed against Sparta but were fatal against Syracuse—and the pervading contrast to Pylos forces the mind back to the difference not only in Athens' fortune but in the nature of her antagonists and thus ultimately to the difference between democracy and oligarchy. And when in the eighth book he goes on in several passages already cited (p. 138) to note Athens' amazing recuperation (a recuperation made possible in part by the slowness of her enemy), it becomes still more clear that the work as a whole embodies a consistent and consecutive view both of the strength and of the reasons for the strength of the several states engaged in the war. Indeed the concept of παράλογος is only a striking means of showing how truth broke through opinion and thus of revealing those basic processes of national change which Thucydides thought would continually recur.

(3) We have hitherto been largely concerned with the concept of Athens' strength, a concept which in turn inspires the claims regarding the scale of the war and particularly of the Sicilian expedition, the contrast between Athens and Sparta, the explanations given for her strength in her naval empire and democratic constitution, and the repeated statements that few persons judged it correctly. Henceforth, on the other hand, we shall be dealing with the opposite and, as it were, balancing concept of Athens'

weakness, a weakness traceable also to her democratic constitution and, so Thucydides thought, accentuated in wartime. As before, the method will be followed of tracing connections of thought between the Sicilian and preceding books, with a view to showing the unity of the work as a whole. But before approaching this crucial topic of Athens' weakness, it will be well to say a few last words of the actual defeat at Syracuse.

As we have seen, Thucydides several times notes that the Athenians met their match only with the Syracusans, who were ὁμοιότροποι with themselves (VI 20.3, VII 55.2, VIII 96.5). The likeness which he observed between the two peoples was apparently a double one, consisting in part of their similar wealth and progressiveness and in part of certain inward traits, such as zest, vigor, and capacity for innovation (VII 21.3–4, 37.1, 70.3). And that he considered these achievements and qualities the result of democracy, is shown by the fact that he joins the words ὁμοιότροποι and δημοκρατούμεναι (VII 55.2). As has been suggested, a great city teeming with manifold activity was probably inconceivable to him except as a democracy, and it is significant that, as Pericles attributes Athens' progress to the energy of her free citizens, so Athenagoras says that the objectives of an oligarchy are ἀδύνατα ἐν μεγάλῃ πόλει κατασχεῖν (VI 39.2). It is natural therefore that the long campaign at Syracuse should have witnessed a gradual change in position whereby the defenders slowly revealed the same qualities as the attackers, and accordingly that, in the account of this change, many motifs of the previous narrative should reappear. Thus at the start, the chief issue is between the ἐπιστήμη of the Athenians and the mere courage of their enemy (VI 68.2, 69.1, 72.4; VII 21.4, 63), the same contrast that is made by the Corinthians, by Pericles, and by the

Spartan generals after the naval defeat of 429 (I 121.4, 142.6; II 87.4). But the fear inspired by the Athenians, like that felt towards the Spartans on Sphacteria, wore away as the contestants came to closer grips (IV 34.1; VI 11.4, 49.2, 63.2; VII 42.3), and though the Syracusans were often beaten, it is said of them, as several times before, that their resolve at least remained unshaken (VI 72.3, II 87.4, V 72.2, but contrast IV 55.3, where after Pylos the Spartans are really shaken in γνώμη). Thus the Athenians (VII 55.2) could make no headway either by revolution (as they had attempted to do at Megara and in Boeotia) or by arms (as they had done against the more backward and immobile Spartans). Then on the introduction of the new ship model with heavier sides, the tide turned (VII 34.7); the Athenians, fighting in a narrow space, could no longer make use of the maneuvers of περίπλους and διέκπλους, so terrifying formerly (VII 49.2, II 89.8); and perhaps the most striking symbol of their utter reverse was when they fought the final battle as a πεζομαχία ἀπὸ τῶν νεῶν, tactics called old-fashioned even at Sybota (VII 62.2, I 49.2).[40]

Their whole defeat then is conceived in terms of the foregoing narrative, but even in matters unconnected with the defeat, Thucydides is constantly invoking ideas expounded earlier. Thus Hermocrates refers to the fact discussed at length in the first book, that the Athenians' skill at sea was not something native to them but merely a result of the Persian wars (VII 21.3, I 90.1, 118.2, 121.4, 142.7); like

---

[40] That Thucydides wrote the narrative of Sybota with the rest of the *History* in mind is shown by the fact that I 55.1, the account of the Corcyrean hostages taken to Corinth, looks to III 70.1, where those same hostages are said to have precipitated the revolution. But the account of the latter is clearly of a piece with the rest of the *History* (see below, pp. 154-55, 159-60, 165). Hence it is not surprising that the descriptions of the battles of Sybota and of Syracuse (I 50, VII 75) have much in common.

Sthenelaidas and others, he taxes the Athenians with misusing a power originally got in the name of liberation (VI 76.3–4; I 77.5, 86.1, 99; III 10); and, like the Corinthians at Sparta, says that after all the Persians were not defeated by the Greeks so much as by the length and difficulty of the invasion itself (VI 33.5, I 69.5). Similarly, Euphemus' defense of the empire rests largely on familiar arguments: that in the Persian wars, Athens had contributed ναυτικὸν πλεῖστον καὶ προθυμίαν ἀπροφάσιστον (VI 83.1, almost an exact echo of I 74.1); that, leaving this argument aside (VI 83.2, I 73.2, V 89), it is ἀνεπίφθονον to see to one's own safety (VI 83.2, I 75.5); that the Spartans had always done their best to keep Athens weak (VI 82, I 91.4 and 7, 140.5); but that it is the latter's nature to be ever active abroad (VI 87.3, the doctrine of πολυπραγμοσύνη, elsewhere expressed in I 70, II 63, VI 18.2). Again, Alcibiades at Sparta, like Archidamus, refers to Athens' revenue as her supreme advantage (VI 91.7, I 81.4, 122), and urges Sparta to a show of energy, the lack of which had been so costly before (VI 92.1; I 70; IV 80.5; 108.6; VII 1.4). Many speeches moreover make use of familiar turns of thought: for instance, that a quarrel seemingly distant may concern one closely (VI 78.1, 91.4; I 68.2, 120.2; III 13.5; IV 95.2; V 69.1); that men's moods change with unexpected circumstances (VI 34.7, I 140.1); that what formerly had been most striven for is now freely offered (VI 10.4, I 33.2, III 40.7); that one must feel καταφρόνησις towards the enemy in action but until then act with φόβος (VI 34.9, II 11.5, 62.3). Such a list of recurrent motifs could be very greatly enlarged, but more significant perhaps are the passages where Thucydides himself reverts to his own previously stated ideas. For example, in I 23.6 and VI 6.1, he makes a similar attempt to give an ἀληθεστάτη πρόφασις, and though the former passage expounding Sparta's fear of Athens as the cause of the war is sometimes taken as later than the Sicilian books,[41] the idea is seemingly quite familiar there. For Nicias can speak of Sparta as a πόλιν δι' ὀλιγαρχίας ἐπιβουλεύουσαν (VI 11.7), and as we have just seen, Euphemus describes the growth of Athens in terms quite similar to those of the Pentecontaetia, itself merely a fuller exposition of I 23.6. Other such passages are: VI 2.1, where he glances at the stories of the poets in the same way that he does in I 21; VI 54.1, the well-known account of the tyrannicides, which, as mentioned earlier (p. 123), may contain a reference to I 20 but in any case shows a close similarity of phrase; VII 29.5, on the destruction of Mycalessus by the Thracians, a disaster of the sort alluded to in I 23.2; and VII 44.1 and 87.4, where he talks of the difficulty of ascertaining facts in the same way as in I 22.3, III 113.6, V 68.2 and 74.3. In sum, not only the analysis of Athens' defeat but the whole texture of the accompanying narrative invoke so many elements from the preceding books, that the reader is constantly aware of dealing with the same mind, the same ideas, and the same methods. That is to say, the unity of the *History* is revealed not only by its consistent analysis of events but by a more subtle consistency of style and treatment. Hardly a page, one could almost say, fails to contain some sentence which in form or idea suggests another sentence elsewhere. The conclusion therefore follows that, by the time he wrote his *History*, Thucydides had, as it were, simplified his thought into a number of fixed, clear patterns, the more important of which centered about the great questions of the war, while others denoted the various things that men would say or do under different circumstances and still others the historian's own methods, and that it is largely from the interplay of these patterns, great and small, that the unity of the work derives.

[41] A. Rehm (above, n. 21) 147.

(4) We come then, finally, to his explanation of Athens' failure, an explanation lodged in his whole estimate of Athenian democracy and thus balancing his opposite appraisal of Athens' great inherent strength. Indeed, it could be said that these two ideas together comprise the main argument of the *History*. The causes of Athens' defeat are set forth in the Sicilian books seemingly in two distinct ways: first, by direct explanation of the errors actually committed by the Athenians and, second, by a contrasting picture of the mistakes avoided by the Syracusans; and since the latter topic is the simpler, it may profitably be treated first. In reading the Sicilian books, it is hard to avoid the impression that Athenagoras stands in the same relation to Hermocrates, as Cleon to Pericles. The parallel of course is incomplete since, in the *History* at least, Cleon appears only after the death of Pericles; nevertheless, in the portrayal of both pairs of men the same contrast is undoubtedly made between sanity and violence, restraint of the demos and popular agitation, disinterestedness and self-interest, and correct and incorrect πρόγνωσις. Thus Athenagoras, like Cleon, is scornfully introduced as πιθανώτατος τοῖς πολλοῖς (VI 35.2, III 36.6, IV 21.3); like him talks with extreme passion, sometimes using very similar phrases (VI 38.2, III 37.1); and resembles him also in practicing διαβολή (VI 36.2, 41.2; III 38.2–3, 42–43; V 16.1), though posing as a watchdog of the people (VI 38.4, III 38.2). Now there is no doubt that Thucydides regarded Cleon as a revolutionary figure, since the Mytilenean Debate is merely a projection of the statement made in the general description of στάσις, ὁ μὲν χαλεπαίνων πιστὸς αἰεί, ὁ δ' ἀντιλέγων αὐτῷ ὕποπτος (III 82.5).[42] Similarly, Cleon exemplifies

---

[42] Diodotus' elaborate attempts to allay suspicion (III 42.2–43) also illustrate the latter half of the clause.

the concluding judgment of III 82.8, repeated in II 65.7 and
V 16.1, that such factional leaders, however much they
spoke of the public good, were in reality acting in their own
interests. Accordingly, the same judgment applies to
Athenagoras, who is in fact pictured as fearing military
preparations at Syracuse lest these weaken the populists
(VI 38.2). And exactly here is to be found the crucial trait
common to the two demagogues, namely, their equal
willingness to endanger their respective cities for their own
gain. As Cleon, buoyed by the popular desire for expansion,
refused peace after Pylos and went on in the campaign of
Delium to risk all Athens' earlier gains—a complete rejection of Pericles' strategy—so Athenagoras closed his
eyes to the menace of an Athenian attack which, according
to Thucydides, had originally every chance of success
because of the lack of preparation at Syracuse (VII 42.3).
There were of course still other reasons for Athens' failure;
nevertheless one reason for it was that Athenagoras' views
were not accepted but that the farsighted Hermocrates
carried the day. In other words, Thucydides is illustrating
in the policies of both Cleon and Athenagoras the possibility, ever present under a democratic government, that
politicians for their own partisan ends may jeopardize a
people's military effectiveness. Now he himself says that
war automatically increases the people's sufferings and thus
sows the seeds of partisanship (III 82.2), but on the other
hand, there is no reason to suppose that he thought that
process of degeneration irresistible. On the contrary, it was
to his mind Athens' essential misfortune that she lacked a
second Pericles to lead the people sanely and to check the
demos, whereas by contrast it was the salvation of Syracuse
to have possessed such a man in Hermocrates. Thucydides
stresses his understanding in very much the words which

Pericles uses of himself (VI 72.2, II 60.5); represents him as, like Pericles, able to rally the people when they were despondent (VI 72.2); and above all, shows him as possessed of the supreme Periclean gift of foresight. Again, he is ready to take swift and bold action based on that foresight, and as Pericles at the start of the war had dared suggest burning and abandoning Attica, so he advocates meeting the Athenian fleet before it had even reached Italy (VI 34, I 143.5). The portrait of Brasidas (cf. esp. IV 81.1) and the unique little speech of Teutiaplus the Elean (III 30) also show how much Thucydides admired this capacity for incisive action. In sum, his estimate of both Athenagoras and Hermocrates bears out what he has previously said of the problem of leadership under a democracy. The conclusion therefore follows that, to his mind, one great reason for Athens' failure in Sicily was that, at the very time when her own actions were embodying the worst possible tendencies of a democracy, the Syracusans avoided those tendencies, achieving unity behind an able leader.

To turn now to his judgment of Athens' policies, it is sometimes said on the basis of II 65.11 that he did not think the Syracusan expedition a mistake. But he says rather that it was not so great a mistake as the Athenians' subsequent failure to support it by the right decisions. Thus he saw in the expedition two cardinal errors, of which the latter was the more costly: first, ever to have undertaken a venture so contrary to Pericles' sound plan of war, and second, once it had been decided on, to have exiled the one man who might have carried it off successfully. To take up these points in order, that he considered the expedition a mistake is shown by his repeated remarks on the Athenians' ignorance of Sicily (IV 65.4, VI 1.1) and by Alcibiades' quite incorrect estimate of the resistance that would be met there (VI 17).

As future events proved, it was Nicias who more correctly forecast the difficulty of the task ahead (VI 20–23). Now Alcibiades carried his proposal by appealing to what he called Athens' very nature as an expanding, dominating state—that is, by the democratic doctrine of πολυπραγμο-σύνη (VI 18)—and when Thucydides himself sums up the motives behind the expedition, he says that the ordinary people expected so to extend the empire that they would henceforth enjoy an ἀίδιος μισθοφορά (VI 24.3). Accordingly, he describes them as possessed of an ἄγαν τῶν πλεόνων ἐπιθυμία (VI 24.4), and says that the entire venture was conceived ἐπὶ μεγίστῃ ἐλπίδι τῶν μελλόντων πρὸς τὰ ὑπάρχοντα (VI 31.6; cf. VII 75.7). There can be no doubt that he is signalizing in these statements the supreme rejection of Pericles' advice, first given in I 144.1 and repeated in II 65.7, that Athens should attempt no foreign conquests in the course of the war. But it is equally important to observe that he uses almost the same words in describing the popular desire for expansion in several other places, namely, of Cleon's refusal of peace after Pylos[43] (IV 17.4, 21.2, 41.4), of the campaign of Delium (IV 92.2), and of the attack on Melos (V 97). It follows that these earlier and less disastrous attempts at expansion fore-shadowed to his mind the great attempt in Sicily, and that as the Sicilian books hold their true place in the narrative as relating the greatest and most intense action of the war, so do they in describing the most dangerous leap of Athenian ambition.

That ambition in turn derived from two sources—the desire of the Athenian leaders for power and the desire of the people for the profits of empire—and both of these

---

[43] The people regretted this error when it was too late (V 14.2), just as they later regretted the Sicilian expedition (VIII 1).

tendencies are likewise continuously observed throughout the *History*. The danger to democracy which Thucydides recognized in the self-interested struggles of politicians has already been discussed in connection with the contrast which he draws between Pericles and Hermocrates on the one hand and Cleon and Athenagoras on the other. It scarcely needs be said that he conceived of Alcibiades also as very largely moved by personal ambition and the need of money. Indeed he hardly ever mentions his policies without noting the mixed motives behind them (V 43.2, VI 15.2, VIII 47.1), and it is significant of his consistency of judgment when he says of him in 411 that he then for the first time genuinely acted in the city's interest (VIII 86.4). Now Pericles in his last speech names four qualities which a democratic leader must possess:[44] he must be able γνῶναί τε τὰ δέοντα καὶ ἑρμηνεῦσαι ταῦτα, and must be φιλόπολίς τε καὶ χρημάτων κρείσσων (II 60.5), which qualities are subsumed in the historian's judgment of Pericles in II 65.8, κατεῖχε τὸ πλῆθος ἐλευθέρως. From the description of the later leaders both in II 65 and throughout the *History*, it is clear that he kept these qualities in mind, considering it, as has been said, Athens' supreme misfortune never to have had another statesman who combined them all. Cleon (as is evident from the Mytilenean Debate) did not understand the true needs of the empire; he also enflamed, rather than checked, the people's dangerous desires. Alcibiades, though gifted with political insight, a strong speaker, and able to lead the people, forfeited his influence because he was neither φιλόπολις nor χρημάτων κρείσσων;[45] and Nicias, though possessed of these two latter qualities (it is for this reason that his ἀρετή is signalized

---

[44] Cf. G. F. Bender, *Der Begriff des Staatsmannes bei Thukydides*, Würzburg 1938.
[45] He tries to prove at Sparta that he is φιλόπολις (VI 91.2), but the irony of the statement is enhanced by the contrast to Pericles (see above, n. 28).

in the end, VII 86.5) lacked the power either of rapid action or of compelling leadership. Only Hermocrates possessed all four essential traits. One therefore sees in this remark of Pericles another strand of unity running forward through the whole work; indeed it runs back to the beginning, since in I 22 Thucydides describes his own speeches as intended to convey τὰ δέοντα (that is, judgments of policy of the sort which Pericles was supremely able to make) and Themistocles too is said to have revealed the same insight (I 138.3) in inaugurating the naval policy, the remoter background of which, as we have seen, is expounded in the Archaeology.

It remains therefore only to say a word of the self-interest and folly of the people themselves, which to Thucydides was the latent cause of all Athens' extremism and, quite specifically, of the great disaster at Syracuse. It has already been suggested that the ruinous policies of Pericles' successors described in II 65 were to his mind merely symptoms of the more fundamental social disturbance set forth in the description of στάσις in III 82-83. War, he says, is a βίαιος διδάσκαλος (III 82.2) which inflames the people and thus makes them the prey of unscrupulous leaders. Pericles himself had warned the Athenians against their own veering moods (I 140.1, II 61.2), and during the plague, which is described as somewhat similar to war in its effects,[46] they were sufficiently demoralized to reject both him and his policies. On the other hand, in the course of his last speech he reassures the people by revealing the full extent of Athens' power, although, as he goes on, he had purposely never done so before for fear lest they misuse it (II 62.1). Thus the historian's estimate of Pericles is that of a stabilizing

---

[46] The ἀνομία which began with the plague (II 53) is attributed to the same destruction of ordinary habits that is noted in III 82.2 as the cause of revolution.

influence against either dejection or overconfidence on the part of the people (II 65.8). Cleon, on the contrary, in the fear inspired by the revolt of Mytilene, fostered their inevitable mood of violence, and likewise after Pylos he played on their contrasting optimism, when (so Thucydides keeps repeating) πλεόνων ὠρέγοντο.[47] The attack on Melos constituted still another departure from Periclean policy, which, as we have seen, was based on the restraint, even the concealment, of Athens' full power, not on its naked revelation. Hence, when Thucydides explains the expedition to Syracuse by saying that the people expected to gain an ἀΐδιος μισθοφορά (VI 24.3) and that they were moved by an ἄγαν τῶν πλεόνων ἐπιθυμία (24.4), the words come as a climax to all that has been said before of their dangerous instability and of the equally dangerous leadership to which it gave rise. Here in fact, to Thucydides' mind, is the supreme weakness of Athens, a weakness which from the Archaeology on is often contrasted with Sparta's one great strength, a way of life which, though rigid and unprogressive, was at least stable.[48] But, it must be repeated, this political weakness of Athens is merely, so to speak, the obverse of her material strength, since both were equally the product of her democratic government. Thus Athens was to Thucydides the strongest of all Greek states in his own time or in the past, because as a naval democracy she had at her command the willing, progressive energies of a multitude of free citizens. But by the same token, she was liable to the most costly errors when, under the stress of popular demands (themselves partly the result of the stress of war), self-seeking leaders held forth dangerous hopes. And when, as in Alcibiades' case, lesser politicians from

[47] See above, p. 157.
[48] I 18.1, 71.3, 84, IV 18.4, 55.1, VIII 24.4.

equally interested motives (VI 28.2) attacked the one man who, whatever his weaknesses, possessed the gift of leadership, the suicidal forces at work in Athens were plain. Alcibiades in Sparta could therefore contrast a democracy based on the whole people, τὸ ξύμπαν, which he said the Alcmaeonids had always striven for, with one dominated by the πονηροί (VI 89.5–6)—the same point which Thucydides himself makes in II 65.5 and which he has constantly in mind in comparing the temperate Athens of Pericles to the destructive city of his successors. It made no difference then if, chastened by the disaster at Syracuse, πρὸς τὸ παραχρῆμα περιδεές, ὅπερ φιλεῖ δῆμος ποιεῖν, ἑτοῖμοι ἦσαν εὐτακτεῖν (VIII 1.4). The seeds of division were planted, and it is certain from II 65 that, had Thucydides finished his *History*, he would have followed to the end that process of disunification which he had already traced in the effects of the plague, in the policies of Cleon, in the brutalizing influence of war itself, in the conquest of Melos, and in the Sicilian expedition.

Thus if one surveys the *History* as a whole, keeping in mind the author's two theses in regard to Athenian democracy—that, on the one hand, it made Athens vastly stronger than her rival in all material ways and in the spirit of her citizens but, on the other, was forever liable to the dangers of political disunion and intemperate leadership—the unity of the work becomes clear. One could say that up to the death of Pericles the first thesis is dominant. It inspires the earlier history of naval power in the Archaeology, the view of the causes of the war in I 23 and in the Pentecontaetia, the great contrast between the two rivals in the speeches at Sparta, the opposing forecasts of victory by the Corinthians and by Pericles, and above all, the Funeral Oration. And as we have seen, the same view of Athens' great strength keeps recurring thereafter in the concept of παράλογος, to be asserted still more strongly in the description of her huge effort at Syracuse and even in the account of her later ability to continue. But with the analysis of the effects of the plague, the self-defense of Pericles in his third speech, and the comparison of him to his successors in II 65, the concept of Athens' poltical weakness has already come into play. Underlying the portrait of Cleon, it is brilliantly analyzed in relation to the more general effects of war in the description of στάσις. Again after Pylos (itself a display of Athenian spirit and, as such, a conscious contrast to the reverse at Syracuse), the popular desire for expansion leads to the loss of Athens' chief gains, and the same desire, as cause of the Sicilian expedition and symptom of the political folly by which Alcibiades was relieved of his command, proved ruinous at Syracuse. Thus the Sicilian narrative, as an account both of Athens' supreme strength and of her supreme folly, draws together the vital strands of the whole preceding work.

III

As was said at the start, it is not the purpose of this paper to discuss in detail the many passages sometimes regarded as of early date, a task largely performed by the scholars mentioned at the end of the first section. On the other hand, it is difficult to leave this question of the unity of the *History* without trying to explain why Thucydides waits until after the Peace of Nicias to expound his view that the Archidamian, Epidaurian, Mantinean, Sicilian, and Decelean wars comprised in fact a single struggle. For his failure to say so at the beginning has been without doubt the principle cause of the whole controversy on when he wrote his work and, from the time of Ullrich on, has afforded the chief argument to those who doubted its unity. To omit minor variations, their view has been that he began his work and had much of the first four and a quarter books completed before he realized that the Peace of Nicias was not the end of the war; that he continued it after 404, going back at that time to alter what he had done in the light of later events; but that he died before completing this process of revision; and that consequently the first books are a medley of early and late passages. As we have seen, it has also been thought by some that he wrote the Sicilian books after 413, revising them at the end of the war, and on that view one should reckon not with two but with three periods of composition, namely, the years just after 421, after 413, and after 404. It need hardly be said that both of these theories are untenable, if the *History* gives anything like as clear and unified an interpretation of the war as has been suggested above. For it is difficult to imagine any man so farsighted that he could anticipate by ten or fifteen years what coming events would teach him. To take a modern example, although we can now see in the battle of Marengo the prophecy of Napoleon's career and in the occupation of the Rhineland the future course of the Third Reich, it is unlikely that a contemporary observer, however keen, would have seen in these events exactly what he saw after Austerlitz or after the invasion of Poland. Accordingly, if throughout the *History* Thucydides draws similar conclusions from widely spaced events, portrays the antagonists as acting consistently, and attributes like ideas and phrases to men speaking at very different times, it is natural to see in these continuing lines of thought only the simplification of retrospect. As was suggested above, by the time that he wrote his *History*, he had apparently reduced his thought to a large, though not unlimited, number of recurrent patterns. If so, however, these patterns inevitably betray one period of composition when the war lay clear before his eyes and he contemplated both early and late events in each other's light. To claim such a limited period of composition for the *History* is not, as has been said, to claim that it was written without earlier notes or wholly consecutively. There can be no doubt that Thucydides wrestled with his material seeking to impose order and shape upon it, and in the struggle of writing he may at times have relied heavily on earlier notes or have inserted new passages somewhat abruptly into a previously written narrative. We cannot conceivably follow this complicated process of authorship. But what we can, indeed must, believe, if the previous argument holds, is that no note was utilized and no passage composed before the whole war and, by consequence, the whole plan of the work were already in his mind. For only that assumption will explain the close interplay and firm consistency of his thought throughout the whole *History*.

It therefore merely remains to suggest why he may not have desired to mention the 27-years war at the start, although he was writing with it in mind. Perhaps three chief reasons could be advanced for the omission: first, that such a statement was unnecessary; then, that it would have violated his practice of confining himself to the period which he is describing; and third, that if he had made such a statement, he would normally have done so in a digression, which, however, was not called for until peace had seemingly been made in 421.

To take these points in order, the view, formerly advanced by Ed. Meyer,[49] that an initial statement regarding the length of the war was unnecessary, has great weight, if

[49] See above, n. 8.

only one assume that the *History* was actually written after
404. When the Greek world had just lived through a long
conflict, there could be no doubt what conflict the historian
was referring to. The only escape from such a conclusion
is to assume that his contemporaries did not connect the
five minor wars of the period—an assumption, improbable
in itself, which is not confirmed by such references to the
separate wars as have been collected from later writers.[50]
For Thucydides himself can in the same breath use the word
πόλεμος of the long war and of its separate phases (V 26,
VII 28.3). Accordingly, to speak as he does of an Ἀττικὸς
πόλεμος or of a Μαντινικὸς πόλεμος (V 26.2, 28.2) did
not mean that he could not also speak of a πόλεμος τῶν
Πελοποννησίων καὶ Ἀθηναίων (namely, the 27-years war).
Like the later Greeks, he used the word ambiguously, and
there is no reason to suppose that his contemporaries did
not do the same. Thus, for instance, it is unnecessary to
conclude with Steup that the statement in IV 48.5 to the
effect that the revolution at Corcyra stopped ὅσα γε κατὰ
τὸν πόλεμον τόνδε means that Thucydides had not yet
achieved the concept of a single war.[51] All one need conclude, as before said, is that Thucydides to the end used the
word πόλεμος both of the long war and of any of its phases.
Hence, considering the reasons advanced above (pp. 132–33,
140–42) for the late date of the Archaeology—namely, that
it broaches the idea of magnitude most fully expounded in

[50] F. W. Ullrich, *Beiträge zur Erklärung des Thukydides* (Hamburg 1846) 9–16;
cf. Patzer, "Problem," p. 18.

[51] Since revolution broke out again at Corcyra in 410 (Diodorus XIII 48), the
passage was written after that date, and apparently some time after, since the
interval between the two revolutions is probably to be contrasted with that at
Megara, which is said to have been exceptionally long (IV 74.4). But even neglecting the latter passage, to say that Thucydides in 410 had not yet grasped the unity
of the war is not only to attribute very little insight to him; it is also to say that
he falsified history when he represented such a view as already existing shortly
after the Peace of Nicias (see above, pp. 129–32).

the Sicilian books and that it also reveals the historical significance of Athens' naval power—there seems not the slightest impediment to taking the first sentence in the *History* as referring to the whole war, which he in fact describes, as we have seen, in terms of the two ideas just mentioned. In 404 the sentence could hardly have connoted anything else.

The second reason for the omission is lodged in the whole nature of his thought. Few historians have doubtless ever relived so intensely the situations and scenes successively under consideration as he. Whether the explanation is to be found in his temperament, in his early identification with politics, in the quickening of memory which exile must have bred in him, or in a combination of all these and other factors, may remain uncertain; but the fact is attested on virtually every page of his work. It seems indeed a principal, if not the only, reason for his whole dramatic procedure of bringing the past vividly before the reader in speeches and descriptions. That being the case, he was undoubtedly absorbed when he began his *History* with the problems and choices confronting Periclean Athens, and was not at that time concerned with the end of the war. It is true that he digresses at times to explain why he thinks as he does about certain crucial questions; nevertheless, as will appear presently, even these digressions are not primarily intended to explain the past or future, but to illustrate some vital force at work in what is to him, at that moment, the present. Here again the point may perhaps be clarified by an example. One of the passages most often adduced as of early date is that in the Archaeology (10.2) where, after observing that the power of a vanished state cannot be judged from the mere extent of its ruins, he goes on to say that Sparta might someday be much underrated on such evidence, whereas under the same circumstances the power of Athens would be thought διπλασίαν ... ἢ ἔστιν. The difficulty is with ἔστιν, since, so it is argued, Thucydides would have written ἦν if he had composed the Archaeology after the end of the war. But (to say nothing of the fact that we do not know when he died and thus how much of the revival of Attic power he may have witnessed), it is unthinkable that he would have evoked the picture of Athens' defeat at the very moment when he is expounding the magnitude of the war and the high condition of the contestants. One would naturally therefore take ἔστιν as an historical present denoting the era then under consideration, particularly since, as Patzer has shown,[52] he uses such presents even of towns the destruction of which he himself notes. In sum, this passage merely brings into sharper relief the whole problem of his failure to mention the 27-years war at the start, and part of the answer to both questions must be found in the nature of his art and of his thought. A man of such absorption in the past and struggling as hard as he to analyze its dominant forces might normally be expected to confine himself (doubtless to some degree unconsciously) to the matter in hand, reserving future events for such a time as they would normally come up.

This observation leads to one final reason why he may have failed to mention the length of the war at the start, to wit, the character of his introduction. The Archaeology is not, properly speaking, an introduction but a digression confirming his statement on the magnitude of the war. When therefore Dionysius of Halicarnassus says that he should have begun his work by tracing events down from the distant past[53]—that is, by joining the Archaeology and

---

[52] See above, n. 19.
[53] *Epist. ad Pomp.* 769–70 R.

the Pentecontaetia—he is misunderstanding Thucydides' method. The latter did not bring in the past to make an imposing façade, nor does he digress on the future merely to relieve the narrative, but when he departs from his theme, it is in order to confirm some important statement which he has just made. Thus although Dionysius rightly sees that the Pentecontaetia is a continuation of the Archaeology, he fails to grasp the true nature of each as corroborative notes, in the one case, on Sparta's fear of Athens' growing power and, in the other, on the magnitude of the war. Now there can be little doubt that Thucydides feels most free to glance at both the future and the past in such confirmatory digressions: at the future, for example, in his estimate of Pericles' successors (which supports the statement in regard to his foresight, II 65.6), his judgment of Archelaus (II 100.2), or his remarks on Decelea (VII 27); at the past in the digressions on Cylon (I 126.3–12), Pausanias and Themistocles (I 128.3–138), the history of Attica (II 15–16), or the tyrannicides (VI 54–59). Hence if he had discussed the length of the war at the beginning, he would presumably have done so in a digression intended to confirm some statement to the effect that this was the longest war in Greek history. As it was, he was concerned rather with the idea of magnitude and mentions the idea of length only in passing: τούτου δὲ τοῦ πολέμου μῆκός τε μέγα προύβη (I 23.1). With his interest in chronology, he would clearly have had to go into the question of length somewhat deeply, and therefore being, as before said, absorbed in the actual beginnings of the war and being delayed, as it was, in explaining the nature and methods of his *History*, he deferred that question until the time when it naturally came up, that is, until the time when peace had seemingly been made. What therefore is usually called the second introduction in

V 26 is only partly such; it is essentially a statement that he is continuing his narrative beyond the seeming peace, together with a digression to explain why the several smaller wars comprise one long war and how long that war lasted. As was said earlier, there is no reason to suppose that this was a unique or peculiar opinion; but, considering the ambiguity of his own and doubtless of his contemporaries' use of the word πόλεμος, it called for some discussion, as it did also from the point of view of chronology. Accordingly it is Thucydides' method, not any previous ignorance on his part, which dictates the place and nature of his remarks on the length of the war. After all, since on any theory much of the first book was written after 404, one might suppose that he would have changed the opening sentences first of all, if he knew that these did not express his full experience of the conflict. As it is, however, the omission is far more readily explained not only by the general character of his thought but, quite specifically, by his normal practice in digressions. Indeed to expect anything else is probably to imitate Dionysius in imputing methods to him which were never his own. But if that is the case, then it is possible to return with greater confidence to the facts set forth earlier and to find in the continuity and uniformity of Thucydides' thought the essential proof of the unity of his work.

INDEX OF PASSAGES

GENERAL INDEX

INDEX OF PASSAGES

❦

Heavy type indicates direct quotation.

I. THUCYDIDES

173

Index of Passages

175

Index of Passages

176

Index of Passages

II
OTHER ANCIENT AUTHORS

Index of Passages

Index of Passages

CICERO

De Divinatione II 144:
p. 91
Orator: pp. 66, 85
12.39, 13.40: p. 60
51.172: p. 61n
52.175: p. 60
57.194: p. 61n

CRITIAS

Sisyphus fg. 1: p. 32n

DEMOCRITUS

Vorsokr. II 68B155: pp.
97–98
B200, 227, 250, 255:
pp. 96–97
B267: p. **13**
B276: pp. 96–97

DEMOSTHENES

De Corona 189, **246**: p.
18n

DIO CHRYSOSTOM

Orationes **52.11 and 13**:
p. **11**

DIODORUS

XII 53: pp. **59–60**, 67,
85
XIII 48: p. 165n
XIII 53–54: p. 137
XIII 62: p. 127n

DIONYSIUS OF HALICARNASSUS

De Demosthene
4 and 6: pp. 60n, 85
39.1074: p. viii
Epistula II ad Amm. 2:
p. 60n

Epistula ad Pompeium
2.8: pp. 60n, 85
3.8–9 (769–770 R.):
pp. 167–169

De Lysia
3: pp. **59–60**, 85
6: p. 61n
8: p. x
De Thucydide 24: p. 60n

ΔΙΣΣΟΙ ΛΟΓΟΙ
Vorsokr. II 90 (pages
405–416): p. 39

Index of Passages

181

Index of Passages

Index of Passages

Index of Passages

Index of Passages

Index of Passages

GENERAL INDEX

✿

For ancient authors, their works, and sections of the *History* see also Index of Passages.

Abstractness, 79–82; in Antiphon, 104–106, 114; and antithesis, 105–112; in Protagoras, 73; and substantives, 14, 104, 106; in Thucydides, 42, 53, 89, 114–117. *See also* Antithesis, Generalization, γνῶμαι

Accuracy of Thucydides, vii, x, 2–6, 11, 26, 35, 36, 39, 42–43, 51–60, 66, 88–90, 112–117, 119–120, 126. *See also* Anachronism, Athens of Thucydides' youth

Advantage, *see* συμφέρον

Aegina, Aeginetans, 124, 137

Aeschylus, 15, 45; Euripides' criticism of, 10; and description of Salamis, 47–48; lack of debate in, 77–78, 81, 88; style of, vi, viii, 69, 83; variation in speeches of, 36

Agathon, 62–63, 67, 85, 86

Agis, 125, 137, 138

ἀγωγή, Spartan, x, 14. *See also* Discipline, Oligarchy, Sparta

ἀγών, 77. *See also* Antithesis, Argument, Debate, Speeches

αἰδώς, 15, 16, 79, 100

Alcibiades, xi, 44, 127n, 138, 156–158; gifts of, 160–162; and πολυπραγμοσύνη, 143, 157; recall of, 138n; ruinous self-interest and extravagance of, 23, 38, 52, 124, 134, 136n; self-justification of, 137; speeches of, x, 27, 51, 130, 132, 143, 152

Alcidamas, 5, 61

Alcmaeonids, 161

Alliances, contrast in Euripides' and Thucydides' view of, 20, 28

Altheim, F., 98, 103

Altwegg, W., 73, 90, 93–94, 96–97, 103

Aly, W., 63, 73–77, 80–88, 90, 91, 97–99, 101, 103–104, 106

Ambition, *see* Alcibiades, Athens, Cleon, Empire, Expansion, Pericles, successors of, Self-interest

Amphipolis, xi, 147

Anachronism, v, 3, 6, 51, 56–58, 86, 87. *See also* Accuracy

Anaxagoras, 3, 97–98, 101

Antilogies, 15, 54n, 70, 73, 77–81, 84, 87–88. *See also* Antithesis, Debate, Dialogue, Protagoras

Antiphon (orator), vi note, viii, 5, 75, 90–92; style of, 58, 63–67, 71–72, 86, 105. *See also* Index of Passages

Antiphon (sophist), vi note, 42, 54, 59, 84, 85, 90–115; Aly on, 73–76, 90, 91. *See also* Index of Passages

Antithesis, 67, 69–72, 74–90, 108–117; in Antiphon (orator), 58, 63, 67, 71–72, 86; in Antiphon (sophist), 54n, 105–107; in Diodotus, 32, 66, 86; in earlier sophists, 67, 69, 84, 86, 89, 105–106; in Euripides, 63, 67, 74–88; and Gorgias, 57–62, 67,

187

General Index

General Index

General Index

Euphemus, 27, 34, 44, 143, 152–153
Euripides, vi, chap. 1 *passim*, 55–56, 68–70, 74–85; and Antiphon, 92–96, 99–101, 115; and Protagoras, 106. *See also* Debate, Tragedy, Index of Passages
εὐσέβεια, 10, 33
Euthydemus, 39
Exile, v, vii–xiii, 1, 43, 50, 53–54, 58, 65, 89, 125, 166
Expansion, Athenian, 139; popular desire for, 155, 157, 162. *See also* Empire
Expedience, argument from, *see* συμφέρον
Extremism, Athenian, 139–140, 159. *See also* Athens, weakness of

Fifth-century thought, 33–34, 95, 109. *See also* Athens, Generalization
Freedom, 17, 25, 137, 143. *See also* Democracy, Discipline

Generalization, ix–x, 11, 34–35, 42, 52–53, 56, 79–82, 88–89, 91–92, 109–116. *See also* Abstractness, Antithesis, γνῶμαι, Style
Generations, conflict between, 16, 43–44, 51, 66
γνῶμαι, γνώμη, gnomic tradition, x, 4, 54n, 91, 104–105, 110–111, 120. *See also* Antithesis, Generalization
Gods, 41, 45, 102
Gorgias, 5, 39, 107–108; Diodorus and Dionysius on, 59–61, 85; emulating poetry in prose, 48, 85–86; style of, its influence and antecedents, 3, 53, 57–75, 82, 84–89, 103, 105–106, 111–112, 115
Greece, Greeks, 20, 39, 53, 56, 84, 96, 110–111, 129–130, 133, 141–144, 146, 148, 152, 160, 168
Grosskinsky, A., 120, 122

Hagnon, 123
Harpocration, 104
Hermae, mutilation of, 125, 127n
Hermocrates, 151, 154–156, 158–159

Herodotus, 46–48, 73–74, 101; piety of, 3; and Protagoras, 80; and Thucydides, contrasted with, 10, 73; and uniform style of speeches, x, 36
ἡσυχία, 13, 14, 20, 27, 143. *See also* ἀπραγμοσύνη
Himera, 127
Hippias, 69, 98, 99
Historical process, *see* Society, development of
History, composition and date of, v–vi, xi–xiii, 2, 9–11, 21, 55, chap. 3 *passim*, esp. 118–128, 131, 133–138, 140–142, 145–147, 151n, 152–153, 160, 162–169; incompleteness of, vi, 121, 128, 161, 163; style of, v–x, chap. 2 *passim*; and Thucydides' absorption in the past moment, xii, 127, 131n, 134, 164, 166–169; unity of, v–vi, ix–xiii, 6, chap. 3 *passim*. *See also* Abstractness, Accuracy, Antithesis, Assonance, Digression, Exile, Generalization, Gorgias, Rhetoric, Style
Homer, x, 9, 32, 77, 79, 110
Homoioteleuton, 60, 82. *See also* Assonance
Honor, *see* καλόν
Hude, C., 130
ὑπόμνημα, 106, 108, 114–116

Imperialism, Athenian, *see* Athens, Empire, Expansion, Pericles, successors of
Individualism, 25, 52, 96, 98–99
Ionia, Ionisms, 8, 63, 68, 104, 113
Isocrates, 5, 61
Ithome, 20, 80

Jacoby, 90, 93–94, 96, 97, 103–105
Jebb, Sir Richard C., ix, 68
Justice, *see* δίκαιον

κακοί, οἱ, 22, 34. *See also* πονηροί
καλόν, τό, 18, 19, 81
Kramer, H., 96

General Index

Law, 14–15, 32, 33, 35, 41, 73, 98–102.
  See also Discipline, Nature, human,
  νόμος, φύσις, Oligarchy, Society
Leontini, 59–60. *See also* Gorgias
Lesbos, 145
Likelihood, argument from, *see* εἰκός
Lysias, viii, x, 66, 109, 116

Mantinea, Mantinean War, xi, 37,
  132, 146, 162, 165
Marchant, E. C., 130
Megara, 131, 151, 165n
Melissus, 39
Melos, Melians, 38n, 39–41, 98, 157,
  160, 161. *For* Melian Dialogue *see*
  Index of Passages Thuc. V 84–113
Meyer, Ed., viii, 122, 164
Mycalessus, 126, 153
Mycenae, 141
Myth, 73, 76
Mytilene, Mytileneans, 12, 30, 131, 145,
  160. *For* Mytilenean Debate *see*
  Index of Passages Thuc. III 35–48

Nature, human: argument from, 11,
  13, 50, 75, 81, 88, 101; recurrent
  tendencies of, 121 (τὸ ἀνθρώπινον);
  trust and distrust of, 14–17, 24, 34;
  vitiated by misfortune, 34, 95. *See
  also* φύσις
Naval power, 4n, 12, 20, 25, 26, 38n,
  135, 140–146, 151–152, 159; historical significance of, 135, 141–142,
  161, 165–166. *See also* Athens, as
  naval democracy; Athens, strength
  of
Navarre, O., 67–70, 82, 87, 110–111
Nestle, W., 27, 93
Nicias, 43, 44–46, 49, 51, 52, 118, 130,
  146, 157; and Euripides, 46; and
  ἡσυχία, 143; and Pericles, compared
  with, 46, 158–159; on Sparta, 153
Nicias, Peace of, v, xi, 7, 38, 44, 62,
  67, 99, 130, 132, 162–165, 168–169
νόμος, 13, 14, 42, 98–100; νόμοι, 17,
  79; ἄγραπτοι νόμοι, 14, 16, 28, 73,
  81; τὰ νόμιμα τῶν Ἑλλήνων, 37. *See
  also* Law, φύσις
Norden, Ed., 67–71, 87, 110–111

Obedience, *see* Discipline
Old vs. young, *see* Generations, con-
  flict between
Old-Attic forms, 104, 106
Old Oligarch, *see* Index of Passages
  Pseudo-Xenophon
Oligarchy, 139; Archidamus on, 56;
  Athenagoras on, 150; attitude of,
  80; vs. democracy, 14–17, 27, 35n,
  81. *See also* Democracy, Sparta
Oratory, 6, 22–24, 40, 42, 53, 66–67,
  73, 88, 108–112, 116. *See also*
  Rhetoric

Parallelism, *see* Antithesis, Symmetry
παράλογος, 26, 128–129, 138, 140–149,
  162
πάρισα, παρίσωσις, παρόμοια, 60, 72,
  105. *See also* Antithesis, Symmetry
Parmenides, 73, 97, 101
Paronomasia, 69
Passion vs. reason, *see* Argument,
  Rationalism
Pattern, ix, xii, 11, 121, 128, 163–164.
  See also History, unity of
Patzer, H., 120, 122, 127, 130, 167
Pausanias the Spartan, 168
Peloponnesian War, 3, 6, 165. *See also*
  War, 27-years
Peloponnesus, Peloponnesians, ix, xi,
  17, 84, 125, 145
Periclean Age, 22, 63, 85–86, 99;
  intellectual temper of, 2, 14, 73;
  late, 71; political oratory in, 3, 12n,
  81; rhetorical and sophistic movements in, 68, 71, 75, 87, 89, 90. *See
  also* Athens
Pericles, 3, 13, 18–30, 49, 56, 64, 68,
  123, 135, 136, 143–145, 150, 161–
  162; confidence of, 23, 26, 135, 136,
  140, 149, 161; on democracy, 16,
  22–23, 56; Hermocrates compared
  with, 154–156, 158–159; Nicias compared with, 46, 158–159; and Protagoras, 3, 68, 76; speeches of, x, 4,
  36, 51–52, 57, 67, 69, 85, 120 (*see
  also* Index of Passages Thuc. I 140–
  144, II 35–46, II 60–64); style of, 19,
  54, 57, 67, 74, 82, 84–85, 115;

191

General Index

dides' judgment on, 126, 127, 161. *See also* Athens, defeat of; Index of Passages Thuc. VI–VII

Sicily, Sicilians, Sicilian War, 43–44, 46, 51, 134, 147, 162; and rhetoric, 9, 68, 72, 74–75, 111. *See also* Sicilian expedition, Syracuse, Index of Passages Thuc. VI–VII

Society: development of, 32, 50; in Antiphon, 102. *See also* νόμος

Socrates, 27, 91; and dialogue, 39–40; in *Phaedrus*, 5, 66; in *Protagoras*, 35n

Sophists, 39, 42, 67–69, 71, 111; early, 5, 72, 76, 87–90, 102, 105–109, 113–115; and individualism, 96; influence of, 100–103. *See also individual names of sophists (esp.* Antiphon, Gorgias, Protagoras), Rhetoric, Style

Sophocles, 10, 15, 16, 34, 36; and Antiphon, 92, 94–96, 99, 102–103, 115; debates in, 64, 77–88; piety of, 3, 102; and Protagoras, 54n, 106; style of, 53–54n, 69, 83, 88, 102, 111. *See also* Antithesis, Tragedy

Sparta, Spartans, x–xii, 12, 33, 35–36, 84, 89, 118–120, 130, 133, 138–140, 146, 151, 152, 161, 166, 168; character of, 13–15, 19–20, 24, 28–30, 36–38, 41, 80, 131–132, 160; Creon, Menelaus, Tydareus portrayed as, 15, 16, 20, 30, 41, 79–81; and Decelea, 134, 137; military reputation of, 19, 132, 140, 144; as oligarchy, 129, 144, 149, 153; as outmoded land state, 135, 140–142, 146, 151; speeches of and at, *see* Index of Passages; strength of, 141–142, 144; Thucydides' portrayal of, 52, 132. *See also* ἀγωγή, Athens, Oligarchy

Speeches: in *Iliad* IX, 77, 79; paired, ix, 73, 75, 78; types of, 17, 18, 21, 35n, 51, 115. *See also* Accuracy, Antithesis, Debate, Oratory, Rhetoric, Style

Sphacteria, xii, 36, 146, 151

στάσις, *see* Index of Passages Thuc. III 82–83

Statesman, qualities of, 18, 46, 51, 158–159. *See also* Hermocrates, Pericles, πρόγνωσις

Stesimbrotus, 54

Steup, J., 57, 125, 130, 165

Sthenelaidas, 36, 118, 152

Strasburger, H., 136n

στρογγύλος, 66, 86

Style, 53–54, chap. 2 *passim*; of early sophists, 69–70, 109, 113; imagistic and poetic, 19, 57, 60–63, 71, 73, 76, 82–84, 91, 104, 106, 112, 115; periodic, 71, 77, 82; pre-Gorgian, 59, 68, 70, 89, 90, 103 (*see also* Gorgias); Sophocles' changes in, 83, 102; of speeches, 56–59, 76, 88–89, 112–117; Thucydides' uniformity and compression of, 4–6, 52–53, 116–117. *See also* Antithesis, Generalization, *History*, Ionisms, Lysias, Pericles, Poetry, Prose, Rhetoric, Sophists

Suidas, 99

συμφέρον, τό, 12–13, 19, 32–35, 40, 43, 51, 56, 75, 81, 87, 109

Superlatives, 126, 127n, 129–140

Surprise, *see* παράλογος

Sybota, 151

Symmetry, 72, 78, 88, 106–107, 111–114. *See also* Antithesis

Syracuse, Syracusans, 44, 51, 124, 135, 148, 150, 155, 162; Athenian defeat at, 44, 126, 129, 138–139, 146, 149, 150–159, 161–162; battle of, 46–49, 126, 129, 133, 148; as democracy, 44, 129, 144, 148–151; expedition to, as mistake, xi, 156, 160; mistakes avoided by, 154–156; Thucydides' visit to, xi–xii, 43. *See also* Athens, defeat of, Hermocrates, Sicilian expedition

τεκμήρια, 9, 66, 74, 87

Teutiaplus the Elean, 156

Thebes, Thebans, 27, 37, 38, 44, 49

Themistocles, 141, 159, 168

Theophrastus, 61n, 85

Thrace, Thracians, Thraceward country, viii, xi, 125, 131, 147

General Index